Reptiles and Their World

To some people, reptiles are scaly creatures whose bite is dangerous or fatal. To others, a reptile is a clean pet that never makes a noise. To still others, reptiles are strange and often small relatives of ancient dinosaurs.

Reptiles really are all this and much more. They are one of the great groups of animals with backbones; a group whose varied and often beautiful members live in many parts of the world and amid varied surroundings. They inhabit the driest deserts and wettest rain forests; they are at home in tiny ponds and in oceans. Some kinds burrow underground, but others spend their whole lives in trees.

This book tells what reptiles are and how they get along in their varied homes. We meet garter snakes in vacant lots, leopard lizards on western deserts, and alligators in southern swamps. We watch turtles lay eggs, see fence lizards defend their home territories, and find out whether snakes can hear. We discover why most reptiles need warmth but dare not become hot, and discover why many kinds are useful to human beings. Abundant illustrations show these creatures at the business of living and enable us to recognize important species.

Miss Pallas is a naturalist who has written about birds, insects, and trees. Dr. Fenton is known as author and illustrator of books on natural history. He has watched reptiles in many parts of North America and has kept several species as pets.

Reptiles
and Their World

By CARROLL LANE FENTON

and DOROTHY CONSTANCE PALLAS

Illustrated by Carroll Lane Fenton

The John Day Company   *New York*

MANUFACTURED IN THE UNITED STATES OF AMERICA

Contents

Page

Cold Bodies and Scales   7

Foods for Reptiles   16

Sight and Other Senses   27

How Reptiles Travel   37

Protection from Danger   47

Finding Mates   57

Eggs and Young Ones   64

Growing Up and Growing Old   73

Winter and Summer Rests   81

Where Reptiles Live   89

Reptiles of Dry Regions   99

Reptiles at Sea   107

Useful Reptiles   116

Index   125

The boa constrictor is a non-poisonous snake 8 to 12 feet long. It ranges from Mexico to Argentina, in South America.

The common iguana is a tropical lizard that is often used as food. It ranges from 3 to 6 feet in length.

Cold Bodies and Scales

THAM, a common garter snake, crawled along the edge of a pond. The spring morning was chilly and so was Tham, for his body never became much warmer than the air around him. When he came to a log he crept along it and then stretched out in the sunshine.

The pond where Tham sunned himself was near New York City. But the kind, or species (SPEE sheez), of snake to which he belonged ranges from eastern Canada to Florida, and westward to Minnesota and Texas. Other kinds live in still other places. In fact, garter snakes may be found from the Atlantic coast to the Pacific, and from Central America far northward into western Canada. Some of these creatures live in woods, pastures, or swamps. Others inhabit dry plains, gardens, or even city parks. Several kinds are found on sea coasts and lake shores, where they often swim and catch little fish.

Tham was about two and one-half feet long. Three yellow stripes ran along his back and sides. Between these stripes he was dark green with black spots.

Garter snakes, like most animals, have two layers in their skins. The inner layer is the *dermis* (DUR miss). The outer layer is called the *epidermis,* a word that means "on the dermis."

7

The dermis contains blood vessels and fibers, as well as tiny particles that give the snake its colors. The epidermis is clear, like cellophane, and is made up of scales that overlap. They are thickened with horny material, but the epidermis between the scales is thin and bends easily. It lets the snake twist and turn or wind itself around other serpents.

Tham's skin was shiny and brightly colored when he first lay on the log. But as days and then weeks went by, he scratched his epidermis on pebbles and scraped it against sharp-edged grass. In time it became so dull that Tham looked worn and old.

As Tham's coat became more and more worn, other things began to happen. First he developed a new scaly layer directly under the old one. Then his dermis produced a special liquid that loosened the old, worn epidermis. This happened all over

Tham, a common garter snake.

the garter snake's body, but it showed most plainly on his eyes. They became so dull, or cloudy, that he could hardly see.

Tham's eyes remained cloudy for several days. The snake spent these days in a muskrat's burrow at the very edge of the pond. He came out only on one rainy morning, when he hunted earthworms. He could smell the worms as they wriggled on the ground, and did not need his eyes to find them. Tham ate five or six big earthworms and crawled back to the burrow.

At last the fluid in Tham's skin dried, and his eyes became clear again. He left the burrow and crawled to the log, where he lay until sunshine warmed his body. As soon as he felt like moving quickly, he slipped into the water and began to hunt frogs. When he caught one, he carried it to the bank and swallowed it without chewing.

A week after Tham became able to see again, he came back to the log. But this time he did not take a sun bath. He crawled beside the log instead, touching it now and then with his tongue. He seemed to be feeling the surface, most of which was smooth.

At last the snake found a place where rough bark still clung to the wood. There he stopped and rubbed his face against the bark. He rubbed and rubbed again till the skin came loose around his mouth. Actually, of course, only the old layer of epidermis loosened. Tham pushed it away from his nose, cheeks, and eyes. This uncovered the new scaly layer, which was so smooth that Tham's colors looked very bright.

The old epidermis came off in one strip that turned inside out. Tham scraped and wriggled and slowly crawled forward, turning back more and more of his old, worn covering. At last it slipped off the tip of his tail and lay on the ground. It looked as if it had come from a snake three inches longer than Tham. The skin had stretched those three inches while he pulled it from his body.

Tham took a half hour to get out of his old epidermis. At the end of that time he was hungry. He crawled away from the log and slipped through the grass at the edge of the pond. Minnows often swam in the shallow water, and frogs often sat there. Tham caught two minnows and swallowed them headfirst. He also tried to catch a frog, but missed it. The frog spied Tham and jumped away just as he wriggled toward it.

.   .   .

Most snakes are good swimmers, and some kinds spend most of their lives in water. Other serpents live on land, where they crawl on the ground or in trees. They move smoothly and make so little noise that people often call them "sneaky." Actually, a snake moves in the only way it can — by crawling. Since it has no legs, it cannot walk or run, as dogs and horses do. It also cannot stand upright, like human beings.

A woman who saw Tham soon after he shed his epidermis said he was wet, or "slimy." But a boy who touched the snake knew better. Tham's skin looked shiny because his epidermis was smooth. Other snakes look velvety and some are dull, like dirt. But no snake is wet unless it has just come out of the water. No snake is ever covered with slime, like the soft, slippery slime that covers frogs and many fish.

The boy who found that Tham was not slimy also noticed that he felt cold. In fact, people often say that snakes are "cold-

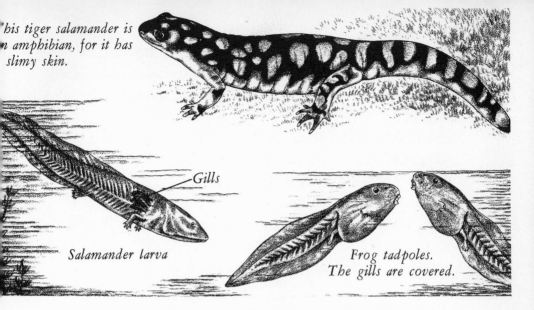

This tiger salamander is an amphibian, for it has slimy skin.

Gills

Salamander larva

Frog tadpoles. The gills are covered.

Amphibians are different from reptiles.

blooded." This separates them from "warm-blooded" creatures such as birds, horses, dogs, and human beings.

Warm-blooded creatures are warm because they use part of their food to produce heat. This heat is found in all parts of the body, but we specially notice it in the blood. When you are healthy, your blood has a temperature of almost 99 degrees. That is hotter than the air on many "scorching" summer days. Dogs, rabbits and horses are a little warmer, and the temperature of a sparrow or chicken may be 108 degrees. This keeps the bird warm, even on very cold winter days.

Tham also uses some food to produce heat, but not enough to keep himself warm. He feels cool to our touch on hot summer days, and on chilly days his skin seems almost icy. He also becomes so dull and stiff that he can hardly move.

11

Of course, Tham is not the only creature with a dry, scaly skin and a cold-blooded body. Other snakes have these things, too. So do turtles, lizards, alligators and their relatives, the crocodiles. All these creatures belong to the big group, or class, of animals which we call reptiles (REP tilz).

Many people think reptiles are related to frogs, toads, mud puppies, and salamanders. These creatures also are cold-blooded, but they belong to the group known as amphibians (am FIB i unz). There are three important ways in which amphibians differ from reptiles:

First, no amphibians have skins covered with dry scales.

Second, most amphibians have soft, moist skins that are covered with slime.

Third, amphibians begin life as partly developed creatures

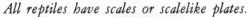

All reptiles have scales or scalelike plates.

This collared swift is a reptile, for it has scales and never breathes with gills.

Scales and plates on the head and neck of a snake.

The cast-off skin, or epidermis, of a snake.

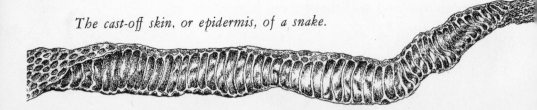

which we call larvae (LAR vee) or tadpoles. Most larvae live in water and swim with their tails. They also breathe by means of gills, not with lungs as reptiles do.

Larvae change in many ways before they resemble their parents. Young salamanders grow legs and lose their gills. Frog tadpoles also grow legs and lose both their gills and their tails. But young reptiles do not make such great changes. From the first they are snakes, turtles, alligators, or lizards. They look and live like their mothers and fathers, and they breathe just as we do — with lungs. If you ever find a "lizard" with gills, you may be sure this strange creature is an amphibian. In fact, it probably will be a mud puppy, for this long-tailed amphibian breathes with gills until it dies.

.   .   .

Many, many kinds of reptiles lived during ancient times. Some were huge dinosaurs that roamed through forests or waded in swamps. Others looked and lived like sharks. Still others flew and soared on skin-covered wings.

These amazing creatures died out ages upon ages ago. Most of the reptiles that are living today belong to four familiar groups. If you live in the South, you may have seen members of all these groups near your home.

1. Turtles and Tortoises. These four-legged reptiles have shells that cover their bodies, though their legs, necks, and heads usually bear scales. Hard shells are made of broad, thin bones. They are covered with special scales that spread out into horny *scutes,* or shields. The big sea-dwelling leatherback turtle has only a bony framework covered with tough skin as much as

13

an inch in thickness. Soft-shelled turtles have lost their tough scales or scutes and the skin that covers their bony shells is soft and leathery.

Although most turtles live in the water, some kinds make their homes on land. The box turtle and desert tortoise are two land-dwelling turtles of North America. Tortoises are land-dwelling turtles that have no webs on their feet.

2. Lizards. Most lizards are four-legged, land-dwelling reptiles, and they never have shells. Some kinds are covered with smooth, shield-shaped scales; in other kinds the scales are rough or spiny. Tails generally are long but legs are short, yet the animals often run swiftly for short distances. Lizards that no longer have legs crawl or burrow. You can tell them from snakes by their ear openings, and by the many rows of scales on their undersides. Most lizards also have eyelids, which snakes never possess.

3. Snakes. We already know that snakes are long-bodied, slender reptiles that have no eyelids, no ear openings, and no

Scales on the shells of turtles have become broad plates called scutes.

Mud turtle   *Painted turtle*

The mud puppy is an amphibian that breathes with gills as long as it lives.

usable legs. The scales on their undersides are so wide that they form only one row. Although most snakes live on land, many kinds are good swimmers and a few inhabit the sea.

4. **Crocodilians.** This group of reptiles contains alligators, crocodiles, and their close relatives. They look rather like large lizards, but they are distantly related to ancient dinosaurs. Crocodilians have large heads and long, flattened tails. Eyes and nostrils are raised on bumps above the head. The skin is covered with leathery scutes which arè large and almost square on the back and underside. These large scutes are reinforced by bone, which makes them very strong.

Crocodilians never shed their epidermis, which becomes larger as the reptiles grow. Turtles also do not change their shells, but some kinds shed the outermost layers of their scutes. Lizards shed the whole epidermis. It may peel off in one piece, or it may be torn into strips. The green anole (a NO le) lizard, for example, tears off strips of its old epidermis and quickly swallows them. You may have seen an anole do this, for these lizards are often sold as pets under the name of American chameleons (ka MEE li unz). They are natives of the southern United States, from North Carolina to Florida and Texas.

15

Foods for Reptiles

LYDRA swam through muddy water near the bottom of a pond. Her short legs and webbed feet made excellent paddles. She swam easily and smoothly, although she weighed almost 40 pounds.

Although Lydra had no name for herself, she was a common snapping turtle. Her big, broad head had a pointed snout, and her jaws were covered with a sharp beak. The skin on her body was black and wrinkled, and scales formed a crest on her tail. The greenish-brown shell that covered her back was 12 inches long, with notches and points along its rear edge. The shell on her underside was shorter and was yellow instead of brown.

Lydra soon swam under a log on which six painted turtles were resting. These reptiles like to sun themselves, and they often sit beside other turtles. But Lydra did not feel friendly, and she never sunned herself. She slipped under the log and went on, without looking at the other turtles.

When painted turtles are hungry they swim about and catch tadpoles, little fish, or insects that live in the water. But when Lydra felt hungry, she stopped swimming and lay on the bottom of her pond. Her colors were almost as dull as the mud.

Lydra, a common snapping turtle.

Tiny water plants that grew on her shell made her look like a stone that had been in the pond for years.

Actually, Lydra lay for only a few minutes before she got something to eat. First some young carp swam toward her, feeding on plants that grew on the mud. The turtle waited until the fish came near; then her head darted forward and snapped up the nearest carp. Lydra cut it into chunks with her beak, since she had no teeth. She gulped each chunk without chewing and soon was ready for more food.

Next came a black water beetle; Lydra swallowed it whole. Then she captured a frog as it darted past her. It was swimming as fast as it could go, but Lydra's head shot out and her jaws snapped before the frog could get away.

After eating the frog, Lydra swam toward the surface of her pond. If a duck or muskrat had passed above her, she would have caught its feet. Then she would have pulled it down to the bottom, where she was able to eat. Like many other turtles, snappers are not able to swallow unless water covers their heads.

On this special day, Lydra found neither ducks nor muskrats. But she did notice a taste that came from a place near the shore. She followed the taste till she found a dead rabbit that had been washed into the pond. A musk turtle was already nibbling the rabbit. He moved to one side but kept on nibbling when Lydra began to eat.

•   •   •

The musk turtle often lay in wait for food, just as snapping turtles do. His long neck moved slowly, but his jaws could open and shut very fast. When he snapped at a beetle or a tadpole, it almost never escaped.

Many other kinds of turtles also lie in wait for food. But the alligator snapping turtle does more than wait; he lures fish into his mouth. This reptile, which is much larger than Lydra, lives in rivers of the South. When an alligator snapper is hungry, it lies on the bottom and opens its mouth. A wriggly bit of pink flesh near the tongue moves round and round, as if it were a worm. But when a fish tries to catch this flesh, the turtle shuts his jaws with a snap. After swallowing the fish, the hungry turtle opens his mouth again.

Soft-shelled turtles (page 19) are covered with leathery skin. Their hind feet have very broad webs, and their eyes are raised above the rest of the head. It ends in a long flexible snout, and the mouth has soft lips that cover a sharp beak. Soft-shelled turtles often lie in mud or sand and wait for food. They also walk on the bottoms of ponds or rivers, turning over stones with their snouts. When they find crayfish or insects, they swallow them whole. Such food is so small that it need not be bitten to pieces.

The snapping turtle is carnivorous (kar NIV er us), for it usually eats animal food. But now and then it feeds on plants, just as cats sometimes eat grass. Soft-shelled turtles may eat water plants, too, and so do painted turtles.

Turtles that feed mostly on plants are said to be herbivorous (her BIV er us). Some are big sea-dwellers such as the green turtle (page 112), which eats floating seaweeds. Wood turtles, which live in fields and forests, like leaves, berries, and mushrooms. Desert tortoises and box turtles are plant-eaters, too, though they sometimes catch insects and earthworms. Pet box turtles seem to like liver once in a while, but their favorite foods are lettuce, chopped apples and carrots, and ripe strawberries.

A southern soft-shelled turtle. The shaded part of the map shows the parts of North America in which soft-shelled turtles live.

Though these reptiles do not chew their food, they taste it as they eat.

Turtles cut their food to pieces before they swallow. But the garter snake has no beak, and his teeth are not shaped for cutting. In spite of this, he is more slender than many of the things he eats. He has had to develop special ways of holding and swallowing food.

Tham hunts by crawling about, and he catches his food with his jaws. They have many short teeth that curve backward. When food is swallowed, it slips past these teeth quite easily. But if a frog or fish tries to escape, the teeth dig into his skin and hold him. If he struggles they hold him more and more tightly, so he cannot get away.

When a blacksnake, or black racer, catches a rat or rabbit, the serpent holds his prey with his teeth. Next he loops his body to and fro over his victim, pressing it against the ground. This keeps the animal from breathing. When it dies, the snake begins to swallow his meal.

King snakes and rat snakes go one step further, and so do big pythons and boas that live in the tropics. All these snakes are constrictors. They catch prey with their jaws, wrap their powerful bodies around the victims, and squeeze, or constrict. Stories sometimes say that constrictors crush their victims' bones and so turn the bodies into pulp. Actually, the creatures are squeezed so hard that they cannot breathe and their hearts are unable to beat. When they die, the snakes uncoil and begin to swallow their food.

Squeezing animals to death is work. It may be dangerous, too, for victims sometimes injure the snakes that are trying to kill them. Poisoning is easier and safer. After one quick bite, the victim dies and can be eaten without danger.

Rattlesnakes are the most famous poisonous reptiles in America. Their poison, which we call *venom,* is made by two glands — one at each side of the head. From there it goes to two long, hollow teeth known as fangs. When the snake bites, its venom is forced through the fangs and into its victim.

A rattlesnake's venom easily kills ground squirrels, rabbits, and other small creatures which the reptile eats. But big rattlers produce so much venom that they also are able to kill large dogs and even human beings. The king cobra, of Asia (page 61), is even more dangerous. This snake, which grows 12 to 18 feet long, produces enough venom to kill an elephant. The cobra bites at the tip of the elephant's trunk or just above the nails on

The Indian python in a zoo has killed a hare and will soon swallow it.

This African egg-eating snake has begun to swallow an egg.

its feet. There the skin is so tender that the snake's fangs can pierce it.

No snake can swallow an elephant or any other big animal. Still, snakes often swallow things that are thicker than their own bodies.

This requires something special in the way these reptiles are built. A snake's lower jaws may look as firm as those of Lydra. Actually, they are loosely fastened to its skull. The bones also are held together under the "chin" by tough material that stretches quite easily. When a garter snake swallows a frog, for example, its jaws spread away from the skull and then stretch apart. At last the snake's mouth becomes big enough to go around the frog.

The two halves of the snake's lower jaw also move separately. First one side holds while the other moves forward. Then the second side holds while the first one advances. This takes place over and over again, until the frog is swallowed. Its body makes a thick lump in the serpent's gullet.

The egg has been swallowed. Its shell will be broken by the snake's backbone.

Many snakes eat the eggs of wild birds or even of hens. The eggs are always swallowed whole. A constrictor, such as the bull snake, first gets the egg into its throat. Then the snake presses its neck against the ground and squeezes until the shell is broken. King snakes let the eggs go into their stomachs and there digest the shells. After that the white and yolk can be digested, too. African egg-eating snakes swallow eggs and break them with points on the backbone.

•   •   •

Other reptiles capture food in many different ways. Alligators and crocodiles, for example, swim after fish and water birds. The reptiles also lie near the banks of swamps or streams, with only nostrils and eyes above water. When animals come down to drink, the crocodile seizes them with its jaws or knocks them into the water with sidewise blows from its tail. The big crocodiles of Africa also hunt animals on land.

Many lizards snap at insects, but others use their tongues. The

A chameleon catching a fly with its tongue.

true chameleons of Asia, Africa, and Europe have long tongues with sticky tips. When a chameleon (ka MEE li un) spies a tasty insect, the reptile creeps slowly toward it. At last the tongue darts out, catching the insect on its tip.

Most lizards are carnivorous, but some kinds eat plants. Chuckawallas in the Southwest nibble fruit, buds, flowers, and leaves. Some iguanas that live on the Galapagos Islands, west of South America, dive into the ocean and feed on seaweeds.

Lizards often use their forefeet to push food into their mouths. But reptiles never catch food with their forefeet, as cats capture mice. Even the huge meat-eating dinosaurs of ancient ages captured prey with their jaws, which had teeth five to seven inches long.

Most lizards and turtles eat every day when food is plentiful. When it is scarce, they do without for days at a time. Species that live where winters are cold also go without eating from autumn until spring.

Snakes seldom eat every day, but they may have one or two meals a week. These meals frequently are large. One day a big python in a German zoo devoured two goats that weighed 67 pounds. Another python ate an 84-pound goat, swallowing it whole. A little water snake weighing 11 ounces swallowed a three-ounce frog. If human beings could equal that record, a 60-pound boy might eat 16 pounds of hot dogs for lunch!

Although reptiles swallow their food without chewing, they digest it slowly. This is one reason why snakes and lizards may not want to eat for several days after they have had a big meal. Reptiles use their food slowly, too. They do not warm their bodies, as we do, and they do not keep moving about. Turtles sun themselves on logs for hours; lizards rest in warm corners; pythons lie so long in one place that they never seem to move.

This Gila monster has stored fat in its thick tail.

One big meal nourishes such a creature for a long time. A few big meals provide extra food that can be stored away in the form of fat. Gila monsters and some other lizards store most of their fat in their tails. Turtles and snakes, whose tails are small, add fat all over their bodies. Stored-up fat can be used when other food is scarce.

People who keep reptiles as pets sometimes forget that they need water as well as food. Meat-eaters get some water in the form of blood, and herbivores such as the chuckawalla get liquid when they eat juicy plants. But most reptiles also have to drink, just as dogs and horses do. This is the reason why zoos have pools or basins of water in reptile cages. You can tell whether a snake is drinking by looking at the back of its head. If it swells and contracts, the reptile is sucking liquid into its mouth.

Desert tortoises are able to go for months without drinking. But when rains fall and fill low places with water, every desert tortoise hurries to a pool. There he drinks as much as he can hold. Part of the water goes into his stomach and then through his body. The rest is stored in a special bladder under the shell that covers his back. The tortoise slowly uses this water after the weather turns dry and there is nothing to drink.

Sight and Other Senses

CROTA crept out of the tangle of dry weeds and grass in which he had slept all night. His body still felt cold and stiff, so he stretched out in the morning sunshine. At first he lay flat on the ground. Soon he tucked his hind legs close to his sides and raised himself on his forelegs. Then he held his blunt head high and began to look about.

Crota was a leopard lizard. This name came from dark brown and black spots on his yellow-brown skin. Pale streaks ran across his back, but his underside was white.

The leopard lizard wore these colors only on bright summer days. When the weather turned cloudy and cool his skin darkened until the spots could hardly be seen. The pale streaks, however, showed plainly on his dull, dark back.

Leopard lizards inhabit dry parts of the West, from Idaho and Oregon to northern Mexico. Crota himself lived in a broad valley between two mountain ranges in Nevada. There were no trees in the valley, but blue-gray sagebrush was common. Bunches of dry grass were scattered over the rocky ground.

As Crota became warm he felt hungry, so he began to hunt for insects. He poked here and there among the grass and under clumps of sagebrush. Now and then he cocked his head and

27

looked upward. Finally he climbed onto a rock. Then he sat with his head held high, waiting for something to move.

This rock was Crota's favorite lookout, for it let him keep watch in all directions. Soon he spied a grasshopper, clinging to some grass. Crota leaped down from the rock, darted forward, and caught the insect between his jaws. The grasshopper was too big to be swallowed whole, so Crota shook it until it broke into two pieces. He blinked as each piece went down his throat. Then he ran back to his lookout. There he sat so quietly that he seemed to be part of the rock.

Although Crota did not move, he was wide awake. He watched grass sway to and fro as another lizard ran past. He saw a car whiz along a nearby road, and noticed that the car was red. Many animals cannot see colors — dogs and cattle can-

Crota, the leopard lizard, on his lookout stone.

not do so. But human beings and birds see colors plainly. So do some kinds of lizards and turtles, and probably certain snakes. Crota was one of the lizards that see the colors of things, as well as their shapes.

Just as the car whizzed out of sight, a brown beetle crawled toward Crota. He let it come quite close before he pounced upon it. Crota began to crush the beetle — but suddenly he spat it out. The insect had squirted a bad-tasting liquid into Crota's mouth. The lizard shut his eyes, shook his head, and rubbed his face with his forefeet. Then he hid under a bush, still rubbing and shaking his head. He acted as if he were trying to drive that nasty taste away.

Crota tasted the beetle, but he also *sensed* it. Scientists say that we human beings have as many as 17 different senses which tell us what is going on in the world, as well as in our own bodies. Reptiles probably have a smaller number. Six senses were all Crota needed in order to find food, catch it, and keep out of danger, but rattlesnakes and their relatives use seven.

Taste was the sense which Crota used to learn that the beetle tasted badly, and should not be eaten. But he saw the insect with his eyes, which gave him the sense of sight.

Crota was typical of lizards that hunt in the daytime. Ground geckoes, which also are lizards, get their food at night. In spite of this difference, both lizards see with eyes that are built on the same general plan. Except for its rounded shape, each eye resembles a tiny camera with a lens and an opening that lets in light. The lens focuses light that comes through this opening,

By day the gecko's pupil closes to a narrow slit or to several dots.

The ground gecko, a lizard that hunts at night.

which is called the pupil. In a camera, the focused light makes a picture on a film. In an eye, light affects the ends of nerves and so produces a message that goes to the brain. When the message arrives, it makes a picture of anything that is seen.

Pupils change size to match the brightness of light. On sunny days the leopard lizard's pupils become small. They let in as much light as the eyes need for seeing, but keep out the rest. On dull days, the pupils grow large, letting more and more light into the eyes. This allows the lizard to see things almost as plainly as it does in bright sunshine.

The ground geckoes' eyes are even more surprising. At night their pupils grow big and round. They let in so much of the very dim light that the lizards are able to see. When day begins, the pupils become smaller and smaller. At last they are only narrow slits or rows of small holes that let in very little light. This protects the rest of the eyes, which probably would be damaged by brilliant desert sunshine.

30

Cats and owls are not reptiles, but their eyes have pupils that become slits. So do rattlesnakes, copperheads, and their relatives. We call such pupils elliptical (i LIP ti kul). Creatures that have elliptical pupils usually hunt late in the evening or at night, as ground geckoes do.

Ground geckoes have eyelids, but some geckoes and other night lizards do not. Snakes also have no eyelids, for their eyes are covered with clear scales. A snake's eyes are always open, even when it is asleep.

Reptile eyes are built on one general plan, yet they see in different ways. The leopard lizard's eyes, for example, are placed at the side of his head. If the lizard wants to look straight forward, he has to turn his head. Since he sees most things with only one eye, it sends a flat (or monocular) picture message to his brain. Each eye also sends its own message, for the eyes see different things.

Vine snakes are slender reptiles that live in Mexico and southern Arizona. The vine snake's eyes are near the front of the head. This allows both eyes to look forward, just as your eyes do. This two-eyed, or binocular, vision produces a picture message that "has depth." Instead of being flat, it shows faraway things behind those that are near, and indicates the distances between them.

Alligators have monocular vision, but their eyes are raised above their faces, and are not at the sides of their heads. Alligators can look both sideways and upward, especially when they lie just below the surface of a pond or stream. Chameleons also have large eyes. Instead of being raised, they bulge out from the head, and turn in all directions. A chameleon can look upward, downward, backward, and sideways. One eye can even look forward while the other peers toward the rear.

Since reptiles cannot warm themselves, they have to know when the weather turns cool. They also need to know when the sunshine is growing so hot that it can make the creatures ill or kill them.

Crota feels cold and heat with his skin, and so do other reptiles. But they probably do not bother to think "This is cold" or "That is hot," as we do. When a reptile feels too warm or too chilly, it simply goes to a shady place or moves into one that is sunny. If the creature still feels uncomfortable, it may hide. It sometimes hides for weeks or months at a time, as we shall find on pages 86 to 88.

Feeling heat or cold is different from feeling vibrations that come through the ground or through water. Crota often felt the *thump! thump!* of horses' feet as they walked through his valley. Snakes also feel the vibrations of hoofbeats, and even the *scrape, scr-r-rape* of insects that dig into the ground. Turtles sense vibrations in water. Lydra can feel a fish or frog swim toward her and get ready to catch it.

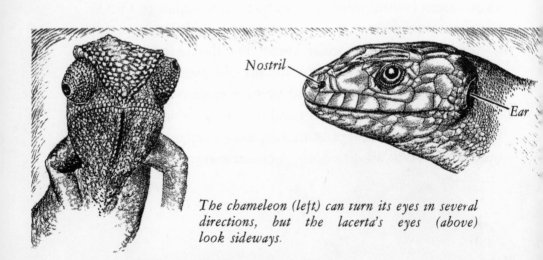

Nostril

Ear

The chameleon (left) can turn its eyes in several directions, but the lacerta's eyes (above) look sideways.

This kind of feeling often warns reptiles of danger. Crota runs away when he feels the vibration of horses' hoofs or of men's shoes that go *clump! clump!* on the ground. Chuckawallas hide when people scramble over rocks. Turtles that are sunning themselves dive into water when footsteps come too near. Blacksnakes "race" to shelter, but rattlesnakes are likely to shake their rattles and get ready to strike. Vibrations warn all these reptiles of danger, but rattlesnakes defend themselves instead of crawling away.

Sounds are made by vibrations that travel through water, through the ground, or through air. These vibrations are picked up by ears, with which many different animals hear.

A lizard's outer ear is like a narrow hole that extends into its head. A thin membrane, called the tympanum (TIM pa num), is stretched across the hole. Horned lizards have tympanums at the surface where they can be seen, but anole lizards have theirs inside the head. When sound waves strike the tympanum it begins to vibrate. The vibrations travel to the inner ear and are passed on the ends of nerves that take messages of sound to the brain.

Snakes have no tube that leads from the inner ear to the surface of the head. Snakes also cannot hear high sounds that come only through the air. But low sounds traveling through water or the ground can be heard. If you know someone whose hobby is hi-fi, ask him to play a sound made by vibrations at the rate of 2,000 "cycles." It will be one of the highest sounds that snakes are able to hear.

Turtles have ear tubes, but their tympanums are thick. These reptiles hear only low sounds that also are loud.

The sense of taste told Crota that the beetle was not good to eat. Box turtles taste strawberries, for they eat ripe ones but take only one bite from berries that are green and sour. Snapping turtles seem to taste dead animals in water. Yet taste is much less important to reptiles than the senses of sight, feeling, and smell.

You can watch a reptile smell when a snake moves its forked tongue to and fro. Many people call it a "stinger" and are afraid

A ball python using its tongue to catch odors.

Komodo dragons are the largest lizards. This one also is catching odors with his tongue.

Head of an eastern diamond-backed rattlesnake.

of it. Actually, a snake's tongue is soft, moist, and harmless. It feels things that are in the reptile's way, just as you can feel things when you put out your hand. The tongue also picks up dust and other small particles that float in the air. They are taken to two tiny pockets called Jacobson's organs which are in the roof of the mouth. They smell odors from the particles. Since snakes also smell with their nostrils, they can explore their surroundings or find food with two smelling systems.

Lizards also have Jacobson's organs. Some kinds do not use them very much, but they are important to monitors. These are long-snouted and long-tailed lizards that live in Africa, southern Asia, and Australia. Some species are shorter than Crota, who is 12 inches in length. Other monitors are two, five, or even six feet long. One, called the Komodo dragon, reaches a length of 10 feet and weighs 300 pounds.

Monitors are related to snakes. This may explain why these lizards have long, deeply forked tongues and why they often use their Jacobson's organs. Monitors resemble snakes in another way, too, for they eat their food whole or in big chunks. One five-foot monitor swallowed a turtle whose shell was more than six inches long.

Rattlesnakes and their relatives use another sense that is a special type of feeling. These snakes are called pit vipers because they have two hollows, or pits, that open between the eyes and the nostrils. The pits are sensitive to warmth — even the tiny amount of warmth that comes from other animals. A pit viper follows its prey by means of smell, using the tongue and Jacobson's organs. But when the snake is close to its prey, the pits feel the heat from its body. Thus they tell the snake just where the victim is, and which way it is moving. They also guide the snake's head as it strikes.

Most rattlesnakes live in North America, but the whole family of pit vipers ranges from Canada to Argentina and through southeastern Asia. Closely related snakes, the true vipers, are found only in Asia, Africa, and Europe. They are venomous, like the pit vipers, but they have no pits. One species, the common viper, is the only venomous snake in the British Isles.

How Reptiles Travel

PILOT BLACKSNAKE was hunting on a hillside. He crept under several bushes and glided across a grassy clearing. Then he glided under some trees. As he slipped between the tall trunks, his tongue moved in and out of his mouth. He smelled odors that came from ferns and dead leaves. Another smell told him that mice had run among the ferns.

Although Pilot was black, he was not related to the common blacksnake. This reptile, which is also called the black racer, is a slender snake with a narrow head and smooth scales that resemble satin. Pilot was not so slender, his shiny scales had low ridges, and his head was wide. He also was a constrictor, for he killed his food by squeezing. Common blacksnakes cannot constrict, though they do loop their bodies over victims and press them against the ground.

When Pilot was young, he was gray with dark blotches on his back and sides. The gray turned dark as he grew older, until his back and sides were black. His underside was yellowish gray with dark blotches, but his throat and lips were white.

While Pilot was hunting, he crawled no faster than a man can walk. He did not travel straight ahead, for his long body slipped this way and that between clumps of grass and curved around bushes. At every curve he pushed against lumps in the ground or against plants, and every push sent him forward. To scientists, this side-to-side movement is known as undulatory (UN dyu la TOE ri), or serpentine, motion. An everyday word for it is "wriggling."

Pilot undulated, or wriggled, along till he came to a big maple. He raised his head and touched its bark with his tongue. Then he began to climb.

When the snake had wriggled on the ground, he used two sets of muscles. One set bent his body from side to side. The other set pulled his scaly skin forward, one section after another. If he had caught a mouse or young rabbit, he would have used

A pilot blacksnake in a tree.

*A pilot blacksnake made this trail
as it wriggled over soft ground.*

still another set of muscles. They would have coiled his body
around his victim, squeezing it until it died.

When Pilot started to climb, he first moved the skin on the
underside of his neck. Muscles pulled this skin forward and
pressed it down against the rough bark. Then the snake moved
the skin below his neck. Soon more and still more skin was
pulled forward. These movements took Pilot up the tree trunk
faster than a man could climb.

In many places, the bark was rough or knots made bumps on
the trunk. There Pilot swung his body, or undulated, just as he
did on the ground.

The broad scales on the snake's under surface helped him
as he climbed. These scales were almost flat in the middle but
bent downward near his sides. They caught hold of ridges on the
bark and helped Pilot pull himself upward. They also kept him
from falling backward as he went over big knots.

The snake climbed until the tree divided into several large
branches. He crawled along one branch and then another. At
last he found a nest that belonged to a mother robin.

Pilot blacksnakes and their relatives eat rats, mice, young rabbits, and squirrels. But the snakes also like eggs and young birds. When Pilot saw the nest he hurried to it and peeked over its rim. There he saw three blue eggs. He quickly picked one up and swallowed it. The mother robin screamed and dived at him, but Pilot snatched another egg. He swallowed it and took the third one before he started back to the ground.

.   .   .

Everyone has watched snakes twist from side to side and coil as if they were made of rubber. They can do this because their backbones are made of many short sections known as vertebrae (VUR teh bree). Some snakes have 300 of these sections, each fastened to the bones before and behind it by easily movable joints. They allow the backbone to bend upward, downward, and sideways, or in all these directions at once.

Common blacksnakes and their relatives, the racers, have tight-fitting skins. These reptiles cannot crawl or climb by moving their skins forward, one part at a time. Young rattlesnakes also have such tight skins that they crawl by wriggling, or undulating. But the skin loosens as the reptiles grow, so the snakes can use both methods of crawling. The skin-crawling method works better and better as the snakes become heavier. Big ones finally stop undulating and crawl only with their skins. This is why large rattlers leave straight tracks when they travel over dusty ground.

Most snakes cannot crawl on loose sand, which rolls when the reptiles pull or push against it. But the sidewinder, of the American Southwest, has overcome this difficulty. So have two kinds of viper that live in Africa and Asia. When one of these reptiles wants to travel, it bends its body into loops which seem to roll sideways. The loops stay close to the ground, but only two or three spots on the snake's body touch the sand at one time. The best way to learn how this kind of movement works is to watch a sidewinder in slow-motion movies.

When a snake climbs a slender tree, it may grip the trunk with a coil of its body and stretch its head and neck upward. Then the front of the body holds tight to the trunk while the snake pulls up the rest of its body and takes another hold. Boa

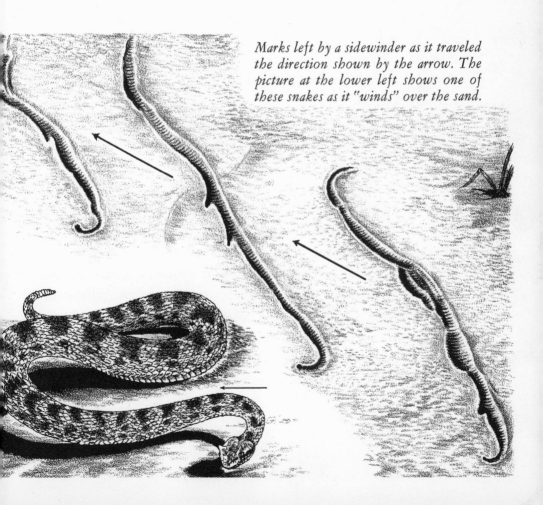

Marks left by a sidewinder as it traveled the direction shown by the arrow. The picture at the lower left shows one of these snakes as it "winds" over the sand.

A collared lizard running on two legs.

constrictors are especially good at this kind of climbing, and so are other boas and pythons. They can also stretch their powerful bodies and catch hold of branches some distance away. In this way the reptiles go from branch to branch and from tree to tree without coming down to the ground.

Most snakes can swim by undulating. Their curving bodies push against the water so strongly that the serpents move forward and do not sink. Wriggling also enables some snakes to burrow in loose ground. The shovel-nosed snake, of the Southwest, seems to swim through dry sand (page 84), just as the common water snake swims in a pond. Yet the shovelnose is much slower than sidewinders on dry sandy ground.

Snakes crawl because they have no legs, but most lizards have four good ones. Lizards use their legs to walk, run, or jump, but they do so in various ways. Long-legged species, such as collared lizards, begin to run on all fours. As the reptiles gain speed, they raise the forepart of the body until they are running on their hind legs. The long tail stretches out behind as a balance for the body.

Collared lizards live in the southern and western United States. Basilisks range from Mexico to South America. They hop and leap through thick, tangled forests, and run on either four legs or two. Sometimes they run short distances on water, going so fast that they do not sink.

Short-legged lizards, such as skinks, bend from side to side as they walk. Species that have no legs at all burrow or crawl, as snakes do. The so-called glass snake is a legless lizard that grows to be two or three feet long. It ranges from Maryland to Florida, Wisconsin, and Texas.

Most lizards climb by means of claws or clinging toe pads. Both geckoes and anole lizards have wide-ridged pads on their toes, which cling to almost any surface. The gecko's toe pads have many little hooks that catch in tiny nicks on walls or even on glass. Warty geckoes can run up walls and across ceilings without falling.

This western skink bends from side to side as it walks.

Anole lizards have toe pads with ridges that hold like hooks, though they do not work quite so well. These lizards are often called chameleons, but real chameleons are quite different. They are tree-dwelling creatures with grasping feet that close around twigs and small branches but are almost useless on the ground. If a chameleon has to steady itself, it wraps its tail around a twig. These reptiles move slowly, even when they are hunting.

A tokay gecko and the underside of its forefoot. Tiny hooks on the ridges hold onto smooth surfaces.

A basilisk running swiftly along a branch of a tree.

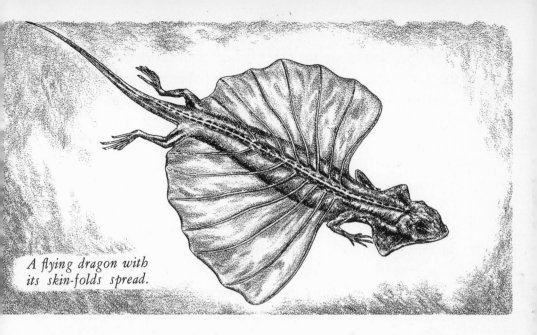

A flying dragon with its skin-folds spread.

Ages ago, there were reptiles that flew with skin-covered wings. Some kinds were no larger than sparrows, but others had bodies as large as turkeys and wings 20 to 27 feet wide. Modern lizards never have wings, but the so-called flying dragon, of southeastern Asia, does have broad folds of skin along its sides. When this lizard leaps from a branch the skin-folds spread and the creature glides to a lower branch or to another tree.

Crocodiles and alligators are able to walk on land, and they often run for short distances. But these reptiles are really water-dwellers. They swim by swinging their tails from one side to the other while the short legs hang close to their bodies. Sea lizards of the Galapagos Islands swim in the same manner.

Most turtles are able to swim, but some are much more skillful than others. Snapping turtles, for example, swim slowly with their blunt, webbed feet but they prefer to walk under

45

water. Sea turtles, on the other hand, swim faster than any turtle can walk. A sea turtle's legs are flattened like flippers or paddles. It swims with its front flippers and steers with the pair behind.

· · ·

When a snake's slender body appears and disappears among grass, the reptile seems to be longer and much more speedy than it really is. Pilot blacksnakes sometimes travel short distances at the rate of six miles per hour. Racers and whipsnakes can crawl at the rate of three or four miles per hour, or about as fast as a person can walk. Other snakes move more slowly. In zoos, the big pythons seem to lie without moving for days at a time.

Although chameleons move slowly, many other lizards are active, and some can dash about so swiftly that they are hard to catch. The six-lined race runner, an American species, can run at speeds of 15 to 18 miles per hour for short distances. In some places it is called the fieldstreak. The sand lizard, or uma, and the gridiron-tailed lizard are almost as speedy. Both live in deserts of the Southwest.

Redback swung his long tail in front of his snout.

Protection from Danger

SCRATCH! SCRATCH! went Redback's claws as he walked along a low branch of an oak tree. His claws made the scratching sound as they dug into the bark.

Redback's full name was red-backed alligator lizard. Although he was only 11 inches long, he resembled a tiny alligator. His head and underside were gray, but the brown bands on his back had black and brownish-red edges. The scales that covered his skin were square, like the scales of an alligator.

As Redback walked, he tilted his head to one side and then the other. This let him look into cracks in the bark. When he saw a beetle in one of the cracks, he crept close to it. Then he folded his legs close to his body and leaped forward. With a snap, he caught the beetle. He swallowed the insect before it had time to struggle or get away.

47

After eating the beetle, Redback walked still farther along the branch. He looked into deep cracks and under leaves. He was trying to catch another beetle. But he would have been glad to find a katydid hiding under a leaf.

The lizard tried so hard to capture an insect that he almost lost his own life. A jay saw him walking and hopped close to get a better look. Then the bird swooped down to a twig just in front of Redback, and struck at him with its beak.

Redback had no place to hide, and no chance to run away. Instead, he swung his long tail forward in front of his snout. He also opened his mouth wide, showing his small, sharp teeth. "Stay back," he seemed to say, "or I'll bite!"

The jay was too large and strong to be harmed by Redback, yet it seemed afraid. After striking once, it backed away. It hopped forward again and then dodged to one side. Finally it darted close and seized the lizard's tail with its beak.

If you hold a dog or cat by its tail, the creature cannot get away. But Redback's tail broke off as soon as the jay caught it. The broken piece also jerked and squirmed, as if it were still alive. The jay shook it and whacked it against the branch over and over again.

While the jay was whacking the tail, Redback himself escaped. He slipped to one side of the branch, and then dropped to the ground. There he hid in a pile of dead leaves until the jay flew away. At last Redback crept into a hollow log. It would be a fine place to stay while the stump of his broken tail healed over and a new tail began to grow.

Many lizards besides Redback have tails that break off easily. Geckoes, legless glass "snakes," and fence lizards do so. When a glass snake's tail breaks off, he is only about one third as long as he was before.

It is important that tails wiggle after they break. A stiff, plainly lifeless tail probably would not interest any bird or beast that is trying to capture a lizard. But a tail that wriggles seems to be alive and worth killing. While the enemy struggles with it, the real living lizard has a chance to escape.

A lizard that loses its tail soon grows a new one, but it is shorter than the one that was lost. Now and then, too, a tail is damaged but does not break off. It hangs on and heals — but while it does so a new tail grows from the wound. After this happens, the lizard has two tails instead of one.

. . .

Even when Redback is not hiding, he looks like rough bark or dead leaves. We say that he is "concealingly colored," or is camouflaged (KAM uh flahjd).

Many reptiles have concealing colors, especially when they are in their natural homes. Sidewinders look like pale desert sand. Copperhead snakes resemble dead leaves that cover the ground under woods. Spotted leopard lizards resemble dry, pebbly ground, and smooth green snakes are quite as green as the grass in which they live. Even bright-colored king snakes are hard to see when they are crawling through woods. Bands of black, yellow, and other colors run around the bodies of these reptiles. The bands seem to cut them into pieces that do not look like serpents at all.

Shapes as well as colors help to conceal, or camouflage, reptiles. Lydra, the snapping turtle, has a rough shell that resem-

A hog-nosed snake swells and hisses as if it were dangerous.

bles mud-covered rocks which often lie in ponds. The vine snake is as slender as many vines. When the reptile is disturbed, it becomes stiff and swings to and fro in the breeze, just as vines often do. Rough scales and bumps cover the back and head of an alligator. They make the reptile look like an old, mossy log when it lies at the surface of the water.

Vine snakes swing to and fro, but many reptiles "freeze" when something strange comes near them. Freezing means that the creature does not move, and so keeps from being noticed. This is especially true if the reptile also has concealing colors. Horned "toads" (pages 99-102) are colored like the ground where they live. We can see them easily when they run, but they disappear as soon as they freeze.

Garter snakes and water snakes also freeze. But if they are discovered, they have another defense. They give off a very bad odor from glands near the tail. This odor bothers some creatures so much that they will not touch the snakes.

. . .

Many lizards are able to change their colors. Scientists once thought the reptiles did this to make themselves look like their surroundings. Thus the familiar anole lizard was said to turn green when it sat among leaves, brown when it went to a fence post, and so on.

Experiments show that this is not true. The common anole looks brown when it is chilly, but turns green when the weather grows warm, *providing the light does not become bright.* In bright light the lizard stays brown until the air becomes very hot. Then the anole turns grayish green, even if it is in bright sunshine. Male anoles also change color when they fight. The one than wins the fight turns green, but the one that loses becomes brown.

The copperhead is colored like dead leaves on the ground.

A diamond-backed rattlesnake shaking its rattle.

Common anoles, which live in the South, are often called "American chameleons." Real chameleons live in Asia, Africa, and on the island of Madagascar. One kind changes from pale yellow green to brown, olive, or dark green with big black spots. Another species flashes red when it is angry; others show patches of blue. These changes sometimes match the lizard's surroundings. Others are very different, and make the chameleons easy to see.

Reptiles with concealing colors escape danger by looking as if they were leaves, bark, or ground. Other species protect themselves by looking as if they were much more dangerous than they really are. The harmless hog-nosed snake does this. If you come close to one of these reptiles, it shakes its tail, swells, hisses, and opens its mouth as if it would bite. This frightens animals and even people, who often call the snake a "spreading adder."

But if the reptile is touched it stops bluffing, rolls onto its back, and plays dead.

Horned lizards have one means of defending themselves which we have not mentioned. When a horned lizard is badly frightened, it forces blood into its head. Much of the blood goes into the thin, skinlike membrane around the eyes. When the membrane breaks, drops of blood pop out and into the face of the enemy. While he blinks and tries to get rid of the blood, the horned lizard runs away.

• • •

Knights of old protected themselves by wearing suits of armor. Alligators and their relatives use this method today. An alligator's largest scales are strengthened by an inner layer of bone. It will not stop a bullet, but it gives protection against the teeth of other alligators.

The snake has shifted into its striking coil, with its neck curved like a big letter S.

Most turtles are covered with bony armor which we call the shell. A baby turtle is soft and is easily killed by almost any meat-eater. But it is hard to kill a grown-up mud turtle or terrapin that has pulled its legs and head into its shell. A box turtle is still safer. The underside of its shell is hinged and closes tightly over the forelegs and head. The hind legs, which cannot be covered, are protected by tough skin and thick scales.

Tortoises are land turtles with high, curved shells and stubby feet that have no webs between the toes. When a tortoise is frightened, he pulls in his head and brings his elbows together in front of his face, while his legs bend back just inside the front of his shell. The opening at the back of the shell is closed by his tough hind feet.

Snakes and lizards do not have shells, but some kinds take positions that protect them. Chuckawallas, for example, hide in cracks between big rocks. There they swell up with air until they cannot be pulled out. Coral snakes and many boas coil their bodies like a hose, with their heads hidden underneath. Ball pythons of Africa and the rubber boa of California roll up into balls instead of flat coils. A ball python protects his head by hiding it in the center of the ball. He does not unroll until he thinks danger is past.

Reptiles that bite or inject venom use these methods for defense, as well as to kill their food. The snapping turtle, for example, bites so fiercely that even human beings often leave it alone. A rattlesnake is still more dangerous, and so are bushmasters, cobras, and many other poisonous snakes.

A rattlesnake rests with his body coiled flat on the ground. His head lies on the coil. When he is disturbed, he lifts his head and shakes the rattle at the end of his tail. The rattle makes a buzzing sound that frightens many creatures away.

But suppose some animal actually attacks the snake. He raises the forepart of his body and holds it in an S-shaped curve. From this position he can thrust his head forward, sideways, or upward. If the enemy comes close, the serpent bites and forces venom into his victim.

Cobras, which live in Africa and Asia, raise the forepart of the body and hold it erect, not in an S-curve. Cobras also spread the skin of the neck into a "hood." Spectacled cobras of Asia (the best-known species), swing toward their enemies and hiss. Now and then the snakes slide forward until they are close enough to attack.

A spectacled cobra (left) has raised its head and spread its hood. A rubber boa (below) has coiled up, hiding its head. The boa's blunt tail is raised as if it were the head.

Some African cobras "spit" venom by forcing it out through their fangs. The venom goes as much as 12 feet and is aimed at the face. It causes pain and blindness for several hours if it gets into the eyes.

.   .   .

There is one more means of escaping from danger, and many different reptiles use it. This is to run, crawl, or swim away. Turtles dive and hide when strange creatures come near them. Pilot blacksnakes and racers dart away through bushes and grass, and so do many lizards. Alligators swim swiftly under-water. Even rattlesnakes will crawl away from danger if they have a chance and are not too much surprised.

This does not mean that snakes are cowards. It also does not mean that they never attack human beings and large animals. Cobras often slide toward people, trying to strike or squirt out venom. The slender mambas, which live in Africa, both attack and pursue people. Attacks are commonest during the season when these snakes mate and protect their eggs.

Finding Mates

BELLOW, an alligator, lay on a mudbank in a southern swamp. The morning sunshine warmed his back and tail, which were covered with scales. The smallest scales were leathery and smooth. Large scales were thickened and strengthened by bone. Most of them also had bumps and irregular ridges, especially on the tail and back.

Bellow was an old male alligator, or "bull," almost 10 feet long. His nose was broad, his body was wide, and only a few of his teeth could be seen when he closed his mouth. These things showed that Bellow was an alligator, not a crocodile. Crocodiles have narrow snouts and bodies. Their lips never cover many of their long, sharp teeth.

Bellow had been asleep, but he was wakened by the *putt-putt* of the motor on a boat. He half-ran, half-slid into the water. He stayed on the bottom for a half hour, until the boat was miles away. Then he swam to the surface and lay with only his nostrils and eyes above water. This let him breathe and keep watch for danger, but kept him from being seen. His nostrils and eyes seemed to be knots of a sunken log.

Bellow often lay in the water for hours, but on this spring day he felt restless. He dived, came back to the surface, and then began to swim upstream. He swam by moving his tail from one side to the other. Bellow used his feet only once, in a place where the water was shallow. There he put his toes on the bottom and pushed himself forward while he swam.

Suddenly Bellow heard the roar of another male alligator. As the sound stopped, Bellow raised his head and filled his lungs with air. His body swelled till the scales on his sides separated and soft skin showed between them. Then he lifted both head and tail and roared. The sound began softly but grew louder and louder. It seemed to shake the water and make trees tremble. A fisherman two miles away heard it easily.

Soon after Bellow roared, he was answered by other alligators. Each one was a male, and each one was telling other males to

Bellow, an alligator, lay on a mudbank.

get out of his way. But females who listened did not worry. The noise told them that several male alligators wanted to become their mates.

A few minutes later, Bellow met one of the other males. Both stopped and made sounds that were halfway between roars and hisses. Then they rushed forward and began to fight. They snapped their long jaws, struck fierce blows with their tails, and rolled over and over. Bellow slashed his enemy's neck, and he struck Bellow so hard that his breath came out with a grunt. Then Bellow bit just back of the forelegs and began to squeeze. The other reptile called *Umph-umph!* in a shrill tone and managed to pull away. Then he swam into a bayou as fast as he could go.

Bellow did not follow, for the fight had made him tired. He floated quietly for twenty minutes. When he felt rested, he swung his tail and began to swim again.

When Bellow had gone almost a mile, he smelled an exciting odor. It came from two glands near the tail of a female alligator, and it told him that she was near. Bellow followed her odor-trail through the water. When he came to her, she made a sound like a loud snore and began to swim away. But she did not go fast or very far. After Bellow followed for a while, she let him catch up with her. This was her way of saying that she would be his mate.

When a male alligator roars, he too produces an odor. It is strong and sweet, and it comes from glands on the jaws. The odor spreads both through air and on water, and it lasts for several hours. It tells female alligators that males are in the vicinity long after they stop roaring.

Many other reptiles use sounds or odors to find mates. Garter snakes leave odor-trails on the ground where they crawl. This odor comes from the skin, and it makes male snakes follow females. Water snakes and several other species also leave odor-trails.

Male tortoises grunt to let females know where they are and to warn other males away. The loudest grunters are giant tortoises that live on the Galapagos Islands, west of South America. These reptiles sometimes become four feet long and weigh 300 to 400 pounds. Their grunts often turn into roars that are almost as loud as the roar of an alligator.

When a male giant tortoise finds a female, he walks round and round her. Then he stands as tall as he can, goes toward her, and

This giant tortoise from the Galapagos Islands grunts when it wants a mate.

The king cobra courts his mate by crawling beside her and touching her head and neck with his tongue.

thumps the front of his shell against one side of hers. While he does this, he may roar with a voice that sounds rather like a horn. This is supposed to please the female, who also may like to be thumped.

Fresh-water turtles also court their mates, or try to please them. These reptiles wander about till they meet other turtles of their own species. Male painted turtles and pond terrapins have long claws on their forefeet. When a male finds a female, he tickles her face with his claws. Other species bob their heads, push, or bite playfully. If both turtles meet in the water, the male may chase the female.

Male snakes court their mates in several ways. A male garter snake crawls close to the female and rubs his chin on her back. Some male pythons scratch their mates with claws that are remains of hind legs. Male common vipers, which live in Europe and Asia, dance in front of the females. Other snakes dance in pairs. They crawl side by side, twist around one another, and swing their heads to and fro. The reptiles sometimes do this for an hour before they settle down to mate.

Many lizards "show off" to their mates, as well as to drive rivals away. These reptiles strut, nod their heads, bob up and down, or spread frills, flaps, and crests of skin. The male anole lizard, for example, has a broad flap of skin (known as a dewlap) which hangs under his chin. The dewlap is bright red between its scales. The male anole can spread this decoration so the brilliant color shows. He spreads it a little and bobs his head as soon as he sees a female. Then he struts toward her.

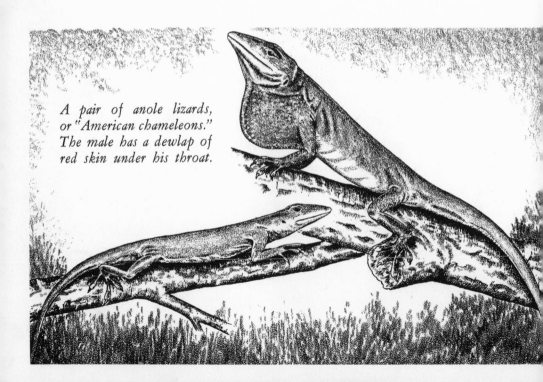

A pair of anole lizards, or "American chameleons." The male has a dewlap of red skin under his throat.

Sometimes another male lizard comes near while the first one is strutting. Each male then spreads his dewlap as much as he can. Next he bobs and struts in front of his rival. If the stranger stays, both lizards fight. As we know, the one that wins turns bright green and stays where he is. The one that loses becomes brown and runs away.

Zebra-tailed lizards have patches of blue on their sides. When spring comes, green patches also appear. The lizards show off these colors by bobbing up and down. Male collared lizards become bright green in the mating season and their black collars show plainly. The males stand high on their legs and look fierce when other males come near. This display also seems to please female collared lizards.

Eggs and Young Ones

LINA, a box turtle, wanted to dig a nest for her eggs. She could have dug in the soft soil under the trees where she lived. But soil is always cool under trees, and Lina's eggs would need warmth to help them develop. She had to find dry, sunny ground for her nest.

Like all box turtles, Lina had a high, curved shell with a hinge on the underside. Her back was dark brown with yellow streaks and blotches. The skin on her legs, neck, and head was black with yellow spots.

Although the turtle was slow and awkward, she hurried as she walked through the grove. In an hour she came to the edge of the trees. Next she crossed a country road, and then she scrambled through a meadow. At last she climbed to a sandy bank where only a few small plants were growing. There sunlight shone on the ground and warmed it. This was just the right sort of place for the box turtle's nest and eggs.

Lina found her sandy bank late in the afternoon. Still, she waited till evening before she began to dig. First she placed her forefeet firmly, so they held up the whole weight of her body. Then she loosened the soil with her hind feet and used them to push it away. She did not dig with her forefeet, and she did not look behind her. The sense of touch in her toes told her what to do while she worked.

The turtle dug slowly and carefully. First her right foot loosened the sandy soil and shoved it away from her body. Then her left foot scooped out more soil and pushed it away. Right . . . left, scoop . . . push she went, over and over again. In an hour she dug a hole three inches deep that widened toward the bottom. Finally she stopped digging and rubbed the sides of the hole to make them smooth. After that she laid her eggs.

Birds lay one hard-shelled egg in a day, or one egg every two or three days. Lina's white, oval eggs were soft, and she laid them one after another. As each egg dropped into the nest, she

Lina, the box turtle, climbed to a sandy bank.

guided it with one hind foot. Then she pushed the egg away to make a place for the next one.

After the fifth egg was laid, Lina scraped some dirt into the nest-hole. She patted the dirt down firmly. She did this again and again, until the hole was full. Finally the turtle turned away and hurried back to her grove. She did not watch over her nest, and she might never see the little ones that were going to hatch from her eggs.

·   ·   ·

Most turtles live in water, but their nests are always dug on land. Frogs' eggs can develop in ponds or streams, and so can the eggs of salamanders. But the eggs of turtles and other reptiles die if they are covered with water. Every reptile that lays its eggs has to put them on land.

This is easy for box turtles and land-dwelling tortoises. But snapping turtles and other water-dwellers have to leave their ponds or streams and dig nests on dry, sunny slopes. Sea turtles come from the ocean and crawl onto tropical beaches. There each mother turtle digs a hole with her hind flippers and lays 50, 100, or even more round white eggs.

Several kinds of snakes also dig nest-holes. Since the mother snake has no legs, she uses her head to loosen dirt. Then she pushes it away with her tail. Other snakes lay their eggs in burrows that were dug by ground squirrels and gophers, or in hollow logs. Each mother snake may use her own log, or several mothers may use the same one. Ring-necked snakes do this, and so do European water snakes. Mother after mother lays in one log, until it contains hundreds of eggs.

Snakes that do not dig holes may hide their eggs under rocks or dead leaves. Pilot blacksnakes do this, though they also leave the eggs in loose soil or old piles of sawdust. Old rotting logs, however, are favorite nesting places for snakes. Lizards like them, too. But some geckoes lay their sticky eggs on walls or tree trunks, and several desert lizards dig their nest-holes in sand.

We know that most birds sit on their nests, or incubate. This warms the eggs and helps them develop into baby birds. Reptile eggs also need warmth, but they cannot get much from their parents. A mother turtle dare not sit on her eggs, for she is too heavy. Like Lina, she leaves her nest and never sees it again after her eggs are laid.

Many snakes and some kinds of lizards do "brood," or take care of their eggs till they hatch. Pythons are famous brooders.

A bull snake guarding its eggs.

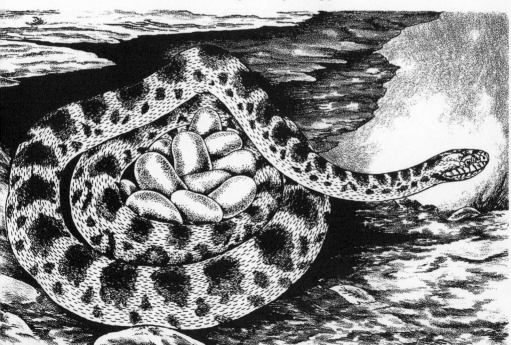

Some kinds lay 80, 90 or more than 100 eggs and then lie coiled around them. Racers, bull snakes, water snakes, and pilot black-snakes also coil around their eggs. Often only the mothers do this, but pilot blacksnakes work in pairs. A naturalist once watched a father and mother of this species take turns at brooding their 44 eggs.

American alligators do not brood, but they take care of their eggs. The mother first piles up mud, grass, and dead weeds on low ground. Next she digs into the pile with her hind feet, making a basin-shaped nest. There she lays from 20 to more than 60 eggs. They look a good deal like long hens' eggs with very thin white shells.

The mother alligator brings marsh grass and other plants in her mouth and drops them on the eggs. When they are covered she crawls to and fro over the nest, making it firm. Then she settles down a short distance away. There she will stay for nine weeks, until her eggs hatch.

The alligator's nest is cool when she builds it. But sunshine that falls on the wet grass and weeds soon makes them decay. Decay produces heat, which warms the eggs. The nest becomes a natural incubator which makes the eggs develop.

Baby alligators are eight to nine inches long when they hatch. As soon as they call *Umh, umh!* the mother pulls the top from her nest. This lets the young ones come out. When all are hatched, the mother takes them swimming. She watches them and protects them, and lets them stay with her during their first winter. They leave her and begin to take care of themselves early in the next spring.

Reptile eggs that are covered with sand or loose soil get

warmth from the sun. Sunshine first heats the ground, and it warms the eggs. They develop rapidly in sunny weather, but in cloudy seasons they develop slowly. Snake eggs that hatch after eight weeks of sunny weather may take 85 days, or almost three months, in summers that are cloudy and cool.

The story of a reptile's eggs begins long before they are laid. At first they are only tiny balls inside the mother's body. They have no shells, no whites, and almost no yellows, or yolks (yokes). For months these tiny eggs do not change. At last, when the nesting season approaches, they become larger. They also start to move through a fleshy tube in which they will change still more.

The eggs grow larger because they fill with yolk, which is mostly stored-up food. The living part of the egg is only a dot on the surface of the yolk. After the mother mates, tiny particles

At the right, a baby snapping turtle has broken the shell of his egg and is crawling out. Below, a pilot black snake is hatching beside an egg that is not fertile.

called sperms go into the egg tube. Soon one sperm combines with every dot and becomes part of the egg. This process is called fertilization (FUR ti ly ZAY shun) because it gives eggs the power to develop into young reptiles. The eggs themselves are said to be fertile (FUR til).

Several things happen to a fertile egg as it moves through the tube in the mother reptile's body. First the dot begins to develop, becoming something we call an embryo (EM bri o). It does not look like its mother or father, but it can keep on changing till it does.

In turtles, crocodiles, and alligators, the fertile egg is soon covered with albumen (al BYU min). This is the watery jelly which we call "white of egg." Next the albumen is covered with shell, which keeps the white and the yolk together. Finally the egg is laid. If it is kept warm and nothing harms it, the embryo then uses the yolk to become a baby reptile.

Eggs of lizards and snakes have no albumen, but they are covered by shells. Each shell is made of tough, stretchy fibers that are coated with chalky white grains. Some lizards put so many of these grains on the fibers that the shell becomes hard. Other lizards and many snakes lay eggs with tough, leathery shells.

Birds' eggs cannot change shape or size, for their shells are hard. The albumen in such eggs contains all the water an embryo will need while it develops into a bird. The egg also contains a pocket of air which the embryo can use.

Eggs of turtles and alligators resemble those of birds. But snake eggs, and those of most lizards, have no stored-up water or air. These substances must be soaked up, or absorbed, through

Freshly laid
(Natural size)

Ready to hatch

A fox snake's egg swells and changes color and shape as it develops.

the leathery shells. This makes the eggs larger and larger as the baby reptiles develop. The eggs also become lumpy and irregular.

The last change in an egg comes when the young one hatches. The box turtle's egg absorbs water and swells until the shell bursts. The baby helps by kicking and by slashing with a cutter, or *egg tooth,* that is on his snout. Other turtles, as well as crocodiles and alligators, have the same kind of egg tooth. But the egg tooth of snakes and lizards is fastened to the upper jaw. Both kinds rub off, or are shed, soon after the little ones hatch.

Many snakes and some lizards do not lay their eggs. We often say that the young of these reptiles are born, like puppies, kittens, and colts.

Still, the process is not quite the same. These reptiles produce eggs inside their bodies, just as turtles do. But after the eggs are fertilized, they are covered with tough membranes, not shells. Each mother also keeps her eggs in her body while the embryos

71

develop into young ones. When an egg does leave the mother's body, it is nothing but a baby reptile covered by the clear membrane. The baby tears the membrane with his egg tooth and wriggles or walks away.

All young reptiles are able to move about as soon as they hatch or are "born." Poisonous snakes can also bite, and their venom is just as strong as their mothers'. Still, it kills only small animals. A baby snake cannot make enough venom to kill a rabbit, a dog, or a man.

When some baby snakes are ten minutes old, they begin to catch insects. Other kinds wait several days before they go hunting. But they never wait as long as turtles, which sometimes go from late summer until the following spring before they eat their first meal. A few kinds even stay in their nest-holes through their first autumn and winter. These reptiles do not walk, swim, or hunt food until they are eight or nine months old.

Growing Up and Growing Old

CON was born in a den under some slabs of sandstone. He began to wriggle soon after he came from his mother's body. Then he jerked his head upward so his egg tooth cut a slit in the membrane that enclosed him. Finally he crawled out of the slit and coiled up beside his brothers.

Con was the last in a family, or litter, of nine prairie rattlesnakes. This species ranges from the Missouri River to the Rocky Mountains, and from western Canada to Texas. Prairie rattlers grow to be three, four, or almost five feet long. Their greenish skin has large brown blotches on the back and smaller spots along the sides. Relatives of these snakes are brown, gray, buff, or even dull red. They are found west of the Rocky Mountains, from Canada to Mexico.

The den in which Con was born was in a high cliff near a river. Mother Rattlesnake lay in the den almost two hours, as if she needed to rest. When she crawled away, Con tried to follow. He stopped when he found a hole under a clump of sagebrush. The hole was small enough to fit a newborn snake. Con slipped in, coiled his body, and soon went to sleep.

The little snake was almost eight inches long and weighed only an ounce. He had a great deal of growing to do before he

would be as large as his mother. Still, he was not in a hurry to eat. For a week he slept all night and most of the day. He left his hole only on bright, pleasant forenoons. He hid in his hole again as soon as the sunshine grew hot.

After nine days, Con shed his skin and his rattle began to develop. He had been born with a bump on the end of his tail — a bump which we call the "pre-button." It broke off when he shed his skin, but a new bump had formed under it. This was the real button, which became the end of Con's rattle. Every time the snake shed his skin he would add a dry section of rattle between the button and his tail.

Con began to eat the day after he first shed his skin. He was coiled at the door of his hole when a little lizard came near. It was hunting for insects in the grass, and it did not notice Con. As it came near him he struck, sinking his fangs into its body. He then waited several minutes, until the lizard was dead. Then Con took hold of it by the head and began to swallow his meal.

We already know that snakes have many small teeth that

curve backward. They hold victims that try to get away, and they help the snakes swallow food.

Fangs that carry venom are not like these holding teeth. A rattlesnake's fangs grow in pairs on the upper jaws. The fangs themselves are long and hollow, and they are fastened to movable bones. This lets the fangs lie against the roof of the mouth, where they stay most of the time. But when the snake strikes, its fangs swing forward. At the same time, muscles in the head squeeze poison glands that squirt venom through the fangs and into the snake's victim.

All this happens very fast — so fast no one can see it. People had to take slow-motion movies to discover just how rattle-snakes bite.

Snake poison, or venom, also works quickly. It kills creatures which the serpent eats, and even begins to digest their flesh before they have been swallowed. Venom also kills creatures that might harm the serpent, for snakes bite to defend themselves as well as to kill food.

Con often felt hungry after he ate his first meal. In the next five weeks he swallowed two young mice and four more small lizards. He also grew three inches longer, shed his skin, and added a section to his rattle. When he shook his tail rapidly, the rattle made a whispering sound.

In October, Con found a crack under a rock in which he could stay through the winter. Grown rattlesnakes often crawl several miles to dens that go deep into the ground. But young ones, such as Con, cannot take such long trips. They stay in holes not far from the places where they were born.

When spring came, Con left his hole and went hunting. Food

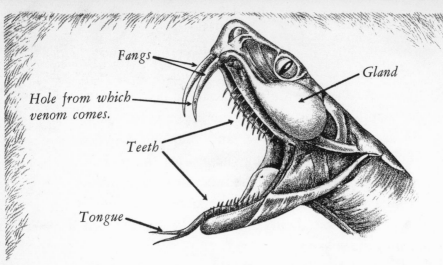

Fangs

Hole from which venom comes.

Teeth

Tongue

Gland

A rattlesnake's head without its skin, showing one venom gland.

was scarce that summer, and he often had to crawl farther than young rattlesnakes usually go. Still, he managed to eat all he needed to grow rapidly.

As Con grew, he began to eat larger and larger food. Sometimes he bit these creatures so hard that he could not pull out his fangs. When this happened the fangs came out of his mouth. This did not bother the snake, for new fangs had begun to grow in his jaws. These new fangs soon took the place of those he had lost.

By the time Con was three years old, he was almost three feet long and had nine sections in his rattle. He was big enough to eat prairie dogs, ground squirrels, and partly grown rabbits. In August he met a female snake and became her mate. They stayed together for several hours, but then they separated. Both went back to their solitary ways of hunting food, sunning themselves, and sleeping under bushes or in holes.

1. *Tail of a newly "born" snake, showing the pre-button.*
2. *Perfect rattle of a four-year-old snake, with button.*
3. *Broken rattle of an old snake.*
How the rattle changes as a rattlesnake grows old.

Con's mate did not bear her babies until the following year. All that time the eggs stayed in her body, developing into young snakes. In September she crept into an empty burrow, where her eight babies were born. The mother stayed with them most of one day and then crawled away. Neither Con nor her little ones ever saw her again.

Con took two more years to become four feet long. In the next four years he added six more inches, for reptiles grow as long as they live. But as years go by, they grow more and more slowly. In Con's tenth year, his length increased by less than a half inch.

People often say that a rattlesnake adds one section to his rattle every year. Actually, a section is usually added every time the reptile sheds. When Con was young he shed three or four times a year, and his rattle grew rapidly. As he became old he shed only once a year. His rattles also lost several sections that had formed in earlier years. First his button broke off when he crawled through some bushes. Then three sections of the rattle were caught between sharp stones. Other sections were pulled off when Con wrestled with another male rattlesnake. After 10

77

years, only five full sections and one that was broken were left in Con's rattle.

By this time, Con had lived a long time for a rattlesnake. In zoos these creatures have lived 12 or even 13 years, but wild ones face many dangers and seldom become so old. Con's mother was killed by a man who found her sleeping beside a stone. Some of his brothers died of disease or froze to death in a very cold winter. Con lived almost 11 years, until he tried to cross a road just as a truck was coming. One of its wheels ran over him, crushing his neck and head.

·　　·　　·

Some kinds of rattlesnakes never become more than 18 or 19 inches long. A few prairie rattlesnakes have been known to reach 57 inches, or almost five feet. They are good-sized snakes, yet they seem small when we compare them with the eastern diamondback. This big rattler, which lives in the southeastern United States, sometimes becomes more than eight feet long and weighs 18 pounds. With its long fangs and its powerful venom, it is one of the world's most dangerous snakes.

Some tropical pit vipers become 12 feet long, and king cobras reach 18 feet. But the non-poisonous pythons and boas grow much larger than any venomous snakes. Boa constrictors are 12 to 13 feet long, and anacondas reach 20 to 28 feet. Another great is the reticulated python, which inhabits southern Asia. It sometimes measures 32 feet in length and weighs 260 pounds. This snake is about 20 inches long when it hatches and grows five feet in its first 20 months. A year-old python is larger than Con was when he died.

The common tortoise of southern Europe sometimes lives more than 100 years.

This fact is worth knowing. People have often supposed that reptiles grow slowly and live longer than other animals. Big snakes seen in side shows are said to be "hundreds of years old." There are stories about alligators that lived 200 or even 300 years.

We now find that those are just stories. The fact is that most reptiles grow rapidly, especially when they are young. Very few species live longer than a man. An eight-foot python may be only two years old, and it probably will die of old age before it has lived 25 years. One reticulated python lived in a zoo for 21 years, and a boa constrictor died of old age 23 years after it hatched. One water moccasin lived 21 years, but very few rattlesnakes become 13 years old. Many small snakes live only four or five years. But the tuatara (TOO a TAH ra), a lizardlike reptile of New Zealand (page 97), sometimes becomes 50 years old.

79

Rough, wrinkled animals always look older than they are. A seven-foot alligator may seem very old, yet its age really is about eight years. It grows a foot a year until it is 11, though after that its size increases more slowly. An alligator 16 feet long is 30 to 40 years old.

Turtles and tortoises have wrinkled skins, and their shells become battered. This makes them look much older than any alligator. Actually, a Galapagos tortoise may gain 320 pounds in seven years, or about 53 pounds a year. One of these reptiles will weigh at least 350 pounds on his ninth birthday. An alligator snapping turtle that weighed 200 pounds lived in a zoo for 57 years. Most smaller species die before they are 40 years old, though a few box turtles have lived 80 to perhaps 100 years.

Tortoises probably become older than any other reptiles. One common tortoise of southern Europe became at least 107 years old and it may have reached 120 years. A giant tortoise about 28 years old was taken to an island in the Indian Ocean. There it lived 152 more years. This amazing reptile reached an age of 180 years!

Winter and Summer Rests

SLEEK, a black racer, lay on a log. The morning sunshine warmed his body and made him feel like moving about. Soon he slipped from the log and glided away to hunt for insects and toads.

Black racers are also known as blacksnakes. They are slender reptiles that grow to be four, five, or even six feet long. They often resemble Pilot (page 37), but their satiny-smooth scales have no ridges. Their back and sides are black, but the under surface is dark gray. The throat and chin are white, with dark spots or irregular blotches.

These are the colors of grown-up racers, but young ones are different. When Sleek hatched he was bluish gray, with reddish-brown blotches and black dots. He kept these colors until the next spring. Then he began to darken, and his spots became hard to see. In the fall, when Sleek was one year old, he was almost as black as a grown racer.

The first autumn days were warm, but the weather soon became chilly. As that happened, Sleek seemed to grow tired of his home in the grassy meadow. Other black racers were leaving the meadow, and Sleek began to follow their trails. He crossed plowed fields and a road, and glided through a woodland.

When he came to the foot of a hill, he turned and crawled toward the top.

The lower part of the hill sloped gently, but the upper part was steep. Beds of rock formed ledges that looked like steps or thick, irregular shelves. Under one shelf was a cave that went far back into the hillside. This cave made a fine den or winter shelter for snakes.

Many serpents besides Sleek were coming to the hillside. Most of these reptiles were black racers, but several were pilot black-snakes. Two were big, thick bull snakes. Their dull white skins had large blotches, and their blunt heads were shaped like the heads of some turtles.

The snakes did not hurry into the cave as soon as they reached the hill. For almost two weeks, they stayed outdoors. They slept under stones or bushes, and sunned themselves on warm after-noons. But day by day the weather grew cooler, and one by

A full-grown black racer has satiny scales that are black above and gray on the underside. Young ones are gray with black and brown spots.

one the snakes crawled into their den. There they coiled around each other in a loose ball. They would stay in this ball all through the winter, and would not come out until spring sunshine warmed the hillside in front of their cave.

.   .   .

We often say that snakes such as Sleek "sleep through the winter," but they really hibernate (HY bur nate). Snakes that hibernate do much more than curl up with their neighbors and sleep. Their bodies grow cold and stiff, and they become unconscious. Their hearts beat very slowly, too, and other changes that are part of living almost come to a stop. If we want a common name for hibernation, we should call it a very deep rest, not sleep.

Hibernation did three things for the snakes that coiled up in the den. First, it let them live without food at a time when they could not go hunting. Second, it kept them hidden away where skunks and other meat-eaters could not find them. Third — and this was most important — hibernation kept the reptiles from freezing. The den was so deep that it got some heat from the ground, just as a basement does. Air inside the snakes' den never grew cold enough to freeze them.

Do you wonder why heat is important to snakes, especially in the winter? The reason is that snakes are reptiles — and reptiles, as we know, are "cold-blooded." This means that they do not produce much heat inside their scaly bodies. In fact, they produce less heat than they need for living. They have to get the rest of the heat they need from sunshine or from their surroundings, such as the air and the ground.

83

Getting heat is easy for the big pythons and boas, and for the other reptiles that inhabit hot, tropical countries. But Sleek has a much harder time, and so do other reptiles that live where winters become cold.

Sleek's body is usually a degree or two cooler than his surroundings. In the early spring they are chilly, and Sleek suns himself to get warm. As summer comes, his body warms up to 70, 80, or 85 degrees. At these temperatures he can hunt, digest his food, find a mate, and dart away from danger. When he is startled he travels as fast as six miles an hour, or 44 feet per minute. His slender body and smooth, gliding movements make him seem to go even faster than he does.

When autumn begins, the weather grows cool, and so do Sleek's muscles. He has to sun himself in the morning before he can hunt, and he rests where the ground can warm his body. He stays away from damp places because they are cool. Dry sand or clay is much warmer, especially on sunny days. He also seems to know that bare rocks and blacktop roads absorb heat,

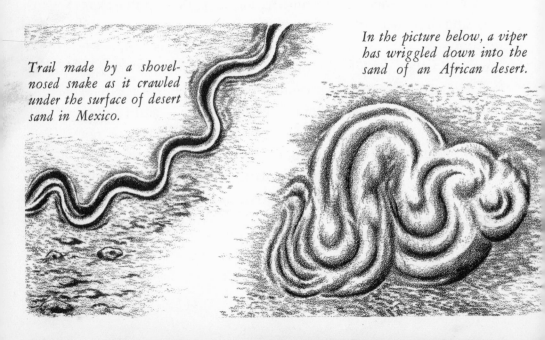

Trail made by a shovel-nosed snake as it crawled under the surface of desert sand in Mexico.

In the picture below, a viper has wriggled down into the sand of an African desert.

and do not cool off until long after sunset. He finds that southern slopes are warmer than ground that slopes in other directions. He often crawls over such slopes just because warm soil feels good on the underside of his body.

At last the weather grows so chilly that Sleek cannot get warm. When his temperature drops to 50 degrees, he grows stiff and can hardly move. Before that happens he crawls into his den and coils up for the winter. There he gets enough heat to keep on living when the ground is covered with snow.

• • •

American alligators live in the South, where winters never become very cold. But the weather does turn so chilly that the reptiles feel stiff and dull. There also may be so little rain that ponds and swamps become shallow. Before that happens, every good-sized alligator digs a bowl-shaped hole in the bottom of a pond. Then he digs a tunnel, or burrow, into the nearest bank. The hole may be eight to 12 feet wide and four to six feet deep. If the alligator is a big one, his burrow may be 60 feet long.

Alligators often wander about from one part of a river or swamp to another. But in October each reptile comes back to his own hole and burrow. He does not grow stiff and cold, like Sleek, and he does not become unconscious. On pleasant days he lies in his pond or even suns himself on land. But he does not catch fish or kill animals that come to drink from his pond. On the coolest days, he goes into his burrow. Though he does not really hibernate, he wants to be sheltered from chill, stormy winds. He also seems to need the heat which his body gets from the ground.

Snakes feel best when their bodies are warm, but they do not like to be hot. Sleek often suns himself on summer mornings, especially if the nights have been cool. But he glides away into shady places as soon as the sunshine begins to feel hot. When the temperature reaches 90 degrees, he hides among rocks and dead leaves or lies on the cool, damp soil under woodlands. Other snakes do this, too, and so do box turtles and lizards. Other turtles dive into ponds or streams, for their water does not become as hot as the air.

Even reptiles that live in deserts take care not to become too hot. Desert lizards hunt food on summer mornings, and so do some kinds of snakes. But when sunshine heats the air and the ground, these reptiles go to shady places. Lizards sit beside stones or under bushes. Desert tortoises hide in piles of rubbish that cover the ground under trees. Large rattlesnakes lie in shady corners or under rocks. Sidewinders and some other desert snakes wriggle down into loose sand. If they could not hide in this way, the summer sunshine would kill them in 15 or 20 minutes.

Lizards hide during the hottest hours of the day, but come out again in the late afternoon. Snakes often wait until long after sunset before they crawl out to hunt food. They leave trails that can be seen the next morning — but by that time, many of the serpents are hiding again.

The desert tortoise is a reptile that cannot stand either great heat or cold. Because of this the creature takes two long rests every year. The tortoise hibernates during the winter, when days become chilly and water sometimes freezes at night. In spring-time the reptile comes out of his burrow. He wanders about, drinks, and eats leaves of juicy cactus plants. He sometimes quarrels with other tortoises, especially if he meets them while he is trying to find a mate.

When summer comes, the desert grows very hot and water becomes scarce. Small plants die or lose their leaves; cactus stems become so dry that they look like wrinkled leather. The tortoise

The desert tortoise rests in winter when the weather is cool. This reptile also rests in the summer, when the weather becomes very hot.

finds nothing to eat or drink, and the heat makes him feel badly. Soon he digs a new burrow or hides in his old one. There he stays until cooling weather and rains come again in the fall. We say that he estivates (ESS ti vates), or takes a long summer rest.

Some crocodiles estivate, too, and so do some alligators and turtles. These creatures live in ponds or streams that dry up during the summer. Before that happens, the reptiles wriggle down into the mud. There they stay until autumn rains cover them with water again.

Since lizards are not water-dwelling reptiles, they do not estivate in mud. But many African lizards hide in deep, sheltered cracks when the hot dry season begins. There the lizards are protected against both heat and drying, which would kill them if they did not rest until the rains return.

Where Reptiles Live

SEL, a common fence lizard, ran over a pile of logs. He dodged into a crack between two of the logs and went to one end of the pile. There he came out and looked around, turning his head upward, downward, and from side to side. Since he saw nothing that alarmed him, he came down to the ground.

Fence lizards belong to the group, or family, of reptiles that are known as swifts. This name tells us that the creatures run and dodge swiftly. They can do this because they have long, strong legs and because they are small. The largest species are not quite 10 inches long, and Sel was less than seven inches. He had a blue-and-black spot under his chin, and two blue patches on his under surface. The rough scales on his back, sides, and tail were gray with dark, wavy cross bands. These colors made the lizard look like bark or dead leaves that lay on the ground.

Sel liked to do the same things over and over again. Every night he slept in a hollow stump not far from the pile of logs. When morning came, he sunned himself on a fence post. Then he scrambled down to the ground and hunted his breakfast. He caught spiders among dead leaves, and found beetles under bark. Now and then he snapped up a cricket in the pile of logs.

Sel almost always sunned himself after breakfast. Sometimes

Sel, a common fence lizard, suns himself on a log.

he sat among dead leaves, and sometimes on a log or a tree trunk. On pleasant mornings, he sat for almost an hour. But when the weather became hot, he did not stay so long.

The lizard acted as if he owned the spots where he rested and hunted. In one way he did own them, for the tree, the stump, the fence post, and the logs were in the place where he felt at home. He had no name for it, but we call it his *territory*.

Sel was a small lizard, and his territory was not large. The hollow stump was in the center, and the pile of logs was near one end. From the logs to the stump was about 20 feet, and the tree and the fence post were 20 feet farther. They were at the edge of Sel's territory.

Of course, Sel was not the only lizard in his neighborhood. A female lived among some old boards in the farmyard that was beyond the fence. Another female stayed among woods close to the tree where Sel liked to rest. These females were not exactly like Sel. One was brownish gray, and one was greenish. Neither female had blue blotches on her underside.

Sel sometimes let these females hunt insects in his territory. But when a strange male appeared, Sel darted toward him angrily. Both lizards faced one another and bobbed up and down, showing their blue patches. When Sel came forward again, the stranger turned and ran into the woods.

One spring day, the female lizard from the barnyard became Sel Fence Lizard's mate. They spent a short time together, and then the female went back to her own home. In time she dug a hole for her nest, and laid 12 eggs in it. Their white shells, which were less than one-half inch long, were oval. They also were very thin.

The eggs hatched on a hot day in August, about 10 weeks after they were laid. One baby was soon caught by a bluejay, but all the others lived. At first they were only two inches long, and they had to eat very small insects. They hunted in their mother's farmyard as well as in Sel's pile of logs. The grown lizards did not know who the little ones were, but neither Sel nor his mate drove them away. It seemed to be all right for very young ones to hunt in grown lizards' territory.

When autumn came, each little lizard found a place to hibernate. Some hid under boards in the farmyard, and several went into the log pile. One baby even crept into the stump where Sel had hidden himself for the winter.

The two lizards did not know about one another while they were hibernating. But when spring came they crawled out of the log and stood face to face. The young one crouched, but Sel raised his head high and shook it angrily. He looked so fierce that the young one turned and ran away.

After that, Sel threatened every young male lizard he met. He was glad to have grown-up females near him, but males always made him so angry that he drove them away.

•   •   •

Most reptiles have small territories, for only a few species travel very far. One of these is the loggerhead turtle, whose picture is on page 108.

Snakes may crawl several miles to their winter dens, but they almost never go far in the summer. A box turtle may stay in one part of a grove except when she goes to lay her eggs. Snapping turtles often spend years in one pond, and painted turtles stay in one part of their stream. So do small mud turtles, whose shells are olive-green or brown. Even American alligators, which sometimes wander from part of one big swamp to another, have small territories. People who watch alligators see the same reptiles day after day in the same pools and bayous or on the same mudbanks.

Every reptile has its own home, and each kind has a set of surroundings in which it likes to live. We call this set of surroundings the reptile's *habitat* (HAB i tat).

The natural habitat of common fence lizards is dry, woodsy country where hiding places are easy to find and insects are plentiful. A barnyard may do as well, especially if it has some piles of old boards. But fence lizards stay away from thick, damp forests, and they almost never go into swamps.

Box turtles and garter snakes are not so particular. Box turtles

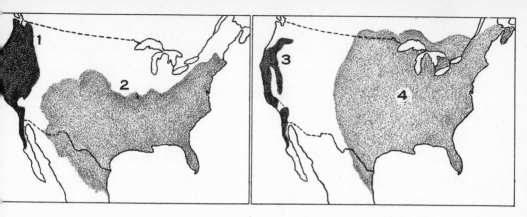

*Ranges of some American reptiles. 1, Western fence lizard.
2, Common fence lizard. 3, Alligator lizard. 4, Common
snapping turtle.*

are found where fence lizards live, but they also inhabit shady
woods, marshy lowlands, and the edges of ponds. Sometimes
box turtles stay in thickets near gardens, where they find plenty
of food.

Garter snakes like Tham are most common in marshes and
moist woods or meadows. But they like roadside ditches and
often live in pastures. They also are found on bushy slopes and
even in dusty fields. Close relatives inhabit dry plains, rocky
deserts, and seashores where the snakes often go swimming in
bays. Some scientists say that garter snakes live in more habitats
than any other group of reptiles.

·   ·   ·

A reptile's *territory* is the place in which it lives. A *habitat* is
the kind of surroundings that are needed by one variety, a
species, or several related kinds. A *range* is the part of the world
in which one of these groups may be found. Sel's territory is

about one fifth of an acre, but the range of common fence lizards is more than 700,000 square miles. It extends from New York to central Florida, and from the Atlantic coast into Utah, Arizona, and Mexico.

This is the range of a single species — the one to which Sel belongs. Another species inhabits deserts and mountains of the Far West, and is common near the Pacific Ocean. The ranges of both species are shown in the left-hand map on page 93.

Although many reptiles have large ranges, they are not found everywhere. Most kinds cannot live upon high mountains or stand long cold winters in the North. This means that only a few species range into Canada. Spotted turtles, painted turtles, and snapping turtles are found in eastern Canada, and so are some copperhead snakes. Prairie rattlesnakes barely reach western Canada, and only a few lizards do so.

Garter snakes are the only reptiles that range from the Atlantic coast of Canada to the Pacific, and far into the North. Some garter snakes have been discovered close to the Arctic Circle. They are not exactly like Tham, of course, for they belong to a different species. His species, the common garter snake, ranges from eastern Canada to Florida, and from the Atlantic coast to Minnesota and Texas.

Many other reptiles have small, or limited, ranges. American alligators, for example, are found only in low, swampy parts of the South, from North Carolina to central Texas. Night lizards live only in the Southwest, and one species seems to inhabit part of a single county in the state of Arizona. Galapagos tortoises live in the Galapagos Islands. Their total range amounts to less than 3,000 square miles.

94

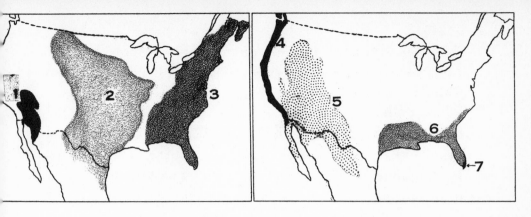

More ranges of American reptiles. 1, Sidewinder. 2, Bull snake. 3, Black racer. 4, Pacific turtle. 5, Leopard lizard. 6, Alligator. 7, Crocodile.

Climates affect the ranges of species, and so do habitats. If a reptile's habitat can be found in only one small region, the range of the species is sure to be small. But if a reptile can live well in many kinds of surroundings, it can range over a large part of a country or even a continent.

Garter snakes are not the only reptiles that have large ranges. Common snapping turtles live well in lakes, rivers, swamps, small ponds, slow-flowing streams, and even roadside ditches that contain a few inches of water. These reptiles range from Canada to Central America and westward to the Rocky Mountains. The soft-shelled turtle also has a large range, though it does not go as far north as the snapper.

The American crocodile is a reptile with a very special habitat. It must be swampy and near sea level, and its climate must be tropical. In the United States these conditions are found in one region — the southern tip of Florida. That is the range of this reptile in the United States, though it also is found from

Mexico to South America and on islands in the Caribbean Sea. There the crocodile's habitat is widespread in marshes along seacoasts.

The granite night lizard is another reptile with a limited habitat and range. Granite night lizards are found only among mountains of southern California, where the ground is made up of granite. By day these reptiles hide under partly loosened flakes of stone. At night the lizards run over the rocks, hunting and eating small insects.

The desert night lizard is a related species that hides under dead and rotting logs of Joshua trees and Spanish daggers. The species once was supposed to be very rare. Now it is known to be common in deserts of southeastern California and southern Nevada, which provide the reptile's habitat.

Species that are closely related may have very different habitats. We have seen this in our two night lizards, for one lives among bare rocks while the other hides under dead, fallen

Two granite night lizards. The map shows the range of this species.

The tuatara lives only on islands near New Zealand.

plants. The Pacific pond turtle is another example. This reptile is closely related to the spotted turtle of the East, which almost never lives in large lakes. Pacific pond turtles often live in marshes and slow-flowing streams, but they also inhabit lakes among mountains. Another relative, the wood turtle, makes its home in moist woods but goes to open meadows to feed. It visits swamps and ponds only in droughts, when food becomes scarce on the hot, dried-up land.

A few reptiles have small ranges because they cannot go to other places where they might be able to live. The Galapagos tortoises are examples of this. Ages ago, ordinary tortoises drifted from South America to these islands in the Pacific Ocean. In time these castaway reptiles had young ones that were larger than their parents. This happened over and over again as years and centuries went by. At last the tortoises became huge creatures that weighed 300 to 500 pounds.

All Galapagos tortoises have small ranges, for all the islands together are about one third as large as the state of Maryland. But while these reptiles were becoming giants, the tortoises on

97

each island became different from those on other islands. On the biggest island, this process went still further. The island has several volcanoes, and the tortoises living on each volcano became different from those on the other mountains. There are now ten species and varieties of Galapagos tortoise. The range of each kind is either one island or a single mountain.

Two reasons explain the tiny range of the lizardlike reptile which we have called the tuatara. Tuataras and their relatives ranged around the world during ancient ages. But they were crowded out or killed by other creatures until only one species was left. It lived in New Zealand, which is about as large as the state of Colorado. That was not a large range, but the reptiles were common in it until settlers from Europe brought cats, rats, pigs, sheep, and goats. Those animals killed tuataras and destroyed the small trees that covered their burrows. The reptiles disappeared from New Zealand's large islands, but survived on 13 small ones where there still are no cats, rats, or livestock. These tiny dry islands are now the whole range of the tuatara.

Reptiles of Dry Regions

CORNU, a horned lizard, ran across the bare, dusty ground. She stopped where the wind had piled loose soil under a clump of sagebrush. Cornu kicked her hind feet and wriggled her body to make a hollow in the soil. Soon she settled down in the hollow and closed her bright, black eyes.

Most lizards have long tails and slender bodies, but Cornu was different. Her tail was short and her body was so broad that she resembled a short-legged toad. In fact, most people call Cornu and her relatives "horned toads" or "horny frogs." Still, dry skins and scales show that these creatures are reptiles.

Some of Cornu's scales were smooth, but many had sharp, spiny tips. Spiny scales were scattered over her back and formed two rows along her sides. But the largest spines were at the back of Cornu's head, where they looked like horns. These spines give horned lizards the first part of their name.

It was eleven o'clock when Cornu hid under the clump of sagebrush. She had spent the morning hunting insects. At first she was rather cool and stiff, but she felt better as the day became hot. Her body worked best at temperatures of 85 to 100 degrees. This was much hotter than the temperature at which Sleek, the black racer, felt comfortable.

Cornu, a Texas horned lizard.

While Cornu chased insects, the day became hotter and hotter. A thermometer on a filling station showed 95 degrees. But that was six feet above ground — as high as the head of a man. Cornu's head was less than two inches high, and her body was still lower. Down there the air became hotter than boiling water, and the ground almost burned Cornu's feet. The heat forced her to stop hunting and hide.

Cornu did not move until late afternoon, when the air began to cool. Then she sat up and blinked her eyes. When a fly came near her, she darted forward and caught it between her sharp-edged jaws. Next she walked to an ants' nest, where she flattened herself on the ground and waited. Dark spots on her tan skin made her look like a dry leaf that had been dropped by the wind.

Cornu waited until the ants began to come out of their home. Then she raised her head and tipped it sidewise, so she could watch the insects. When they came near, down went her head and out shot her sticky tongue. She caught an ant, swallowed it quickly, and then captured another. Cornu swallowed 20 ants before they stopped coming toward her.

As the sun sank low, the air cooled more and more rapidly. Before the ground became cool, too, Cornu ran to a bank of loose sand. She dug into the bank with her feet and pushed from side to side with her body. Soon she was down in the sand, which covered her tail, her back, and most of her head. This hid her from creatures that hunted at night. The sand also made a blanket that would keep her warm until morning.

On summer nights, Cornu needed only a thin blanket of sand. In the autumn, however, she would dig down to a depth of four, five, or six inches. Then she would cover herself and hibernate. Five or six inches of sand would keep her from freezing on any winter day.

Cornu dug another deep hole in June, but this one was a nest. She laid more than 20 yellowish eggs, each almost a half-inch long. Cornu covered them with loose soil and went away, for the ground was warm enough to make her eggs develop. When the little ones hatched, late in July, they dug their way out of the sand and took care of themselves.

Cornu belonged to the species known as the Texas horned lizard. It ranges from Nebraska to northwestern Mexico and is especially common in Texas. There it is often seen on dry grassy plains, but also lives in pastures and in towns.

Several other kinds of horned lizards are found in various parts of the West. They are four to about six inches long, and their colors range from pink to tan, reddish brown, or black.

The regal horned "toad" (really a lizard) is a desert species.

Some kinds live among woods and mountains, but others like dry plains, and several inhabit deserts. Although some kinds dig nest-holes and lay eggs, others bear their young alive. Like snakes, the baby lizards are covered with thin, clear membranes that split and let the little ones creep out. They are shaped like their mothers, but their "horns" have just begun to develop and their skins seem smooth.

. . .

People from rainy lands often think that deserts are bare and lifeless. Trees are seen in only a few low places, and grass grows in little tufts that do not cover the ground. Bushes are small, and many have leaves that are bluish gray instead of green. Some regions are covered with loose sand, which is blown to and fro by the wind, or is piled up in hills called dunes. Other places are covered with a white substance known as alkali (AL kuh lye). When whirlwinds cross alkali deserts, they carry powdery dust high into the air.

Still, deserts are not lifeless, even though they seem to be bare. Plants always grow, and insects live among them. Plants and insects make food for birds, as well as for furry beasts and for reptiles. Most of these creatures are related to species that inhabit regions where there is plenty of rain. Yet many desert-dwellers often fit their surroundings so well that they cannot live in moist places.

Two desert lizards with light-colored skins.

Sand lizard, or
Colorado uma

Zebra-tailed lizard

Turtles do not live on deserts, though some species swim in rivers that flow through bare, dry country. But we know that the desert tortoise is found in some of the hottest, driest parts of North America. Tortoises get along very well by drinking and eating when there is water. Then, when the dry season comes, the reptiles estivate in their burrows. An estivating tortoise does not need water. He also stays cool, though temperatures out on the desert may be hotter than 115 degrees.

Snakes are found on the desert, but they are not common. Snakes live best in warm, moist regions and in the hot tropics. Most desert serpents also are smaller than their relatives that live where there is plenty of rain. Desert diamond-backed rattlesnakes, for example, usually are two to three feet shorter than the longest diamondbacks of the Southeast. In mild weather, desert rattlers hunt in the morning and late afternoon. But when summer comes, the snakes lie in cool corners during the daytime and hunt for food at night.

The sidewinder is also a night-hunter that hides during the day. When morning comes, the sidewinder coils and shakes his body from side to side. This digs away the sand beneath him and pushes it over his back. Thus the snake covers himself with a layer of sand that protects him from the heat. Desert vipers of Africa also cover themselves with sand.

The commonest desert reptiles are lizards, which seem to like hot, dry surroundings. It is true that some kinds inhabit forests, while others live near swampy streams, and one species often swims in the ocean. Still, most lizards inhabit dry places, and many make their homes in deserts.

We have found that Cornu needs heat, though she hides in

The spiny mastigure belongs to a group of lizards that soak up dew or light rain when it falls on their skins.

the shade on very hot days. But the zebra-tailed lizard does better. He runs over ground that is much too hot for horned lizards. He often runs here and there to catch insects when all other reptiles are hiding.

Horned lizards never drink, for they get all the moisture they need by eating juicy insects. The chuckawalla gets liquid from plants. Other species lap up droplets of dew or drink after desert rains. The mastigures of Asia and Africa use a still easier method. These lizards soak up water when dew or rain falls on their skins.

Many desert reptiles have lighter colors than their relatives in moist regions. Horned lizards that live in very dry places are yellowish, pink, or a very light gray. Desert diamond-backed rattlesnakes are much lighter than eastern diamondbacks. Sand lizards are pale, too, and so are zebra-tailed lizards, except for the black rings around their tails.

No one knows why desert reptiles develop their light colors. But we do know that they are useful. Dark colors absorb, or take up, heat, but pale hues do not. This means that a light-colored lizard or snake does not become as hot as it would if its skin were dark. You can prove this by laying a black paper and a white one on the ground in bright sunshine. After a half hour, you can easily feel that the white paper is not nearly so warm as the black.

Since the ground in many deserts is pale, light colors help to conceal reptiles. Sidewinders look like sand, leopard lizards resemble pebbly ground, and the whitish pallid rattlesnake is colored like the rocks among which it hides. Most surprising of all is a species of horned lizard that ranges from Idaho to Mexico. Where the ground is pink, this reptile is pink with spots that match white pebbles. On brown soil, the general color is brown. On deserts covered with black lava or cinders from volcanoes, this species is dark gray or black. The skin also has gray and yellow markings which look like small plants called lichens (LY kens) growing on the rocks.

Reptiles at Sea

A LOGGERHEAD TURTLE was floating in the Atlantic Ocean. His eyes were shut and his legs hung down loosely, for he was asleep.

The turtle slept a long time — more than three hours. When he woke up, he raised his head and looked around him. He saw only the sea water, the sky, and some clouds that were overhead. Then suddenly he felt like swimming. He sank below the surface and moved his forelegs, which really were long flippers. The turtle pushed his flippers forward and upward, higher than his head. Then he pulled them downward and backward. He looked as if he were flying lazily through the sea.

Loggerhead seemed to be lazy because he was not in a hurry. When he was frightened he moved his flippers much faster — fast enough to travel at speeds of 18 or 20 miles per hour. He used his paddle-shaped hind legs for steering. Sometimes he also spread them out sideways. This made them work as brakes, enabling Loggerhead to stop.

Most turtles that swim in the ocean are larger than their relatives in lakes and rivers. Loggerhead's shell was almost three feet long, and he weighed 250 pounds. Broad, smooth plates covered his back and underside, as well as his big, thick head.

A loggerhead turtle diving.

His beak had curved edges and was "hooked," like the beak of a hawk or eagle.

Although Loggerhead was very large, he was only 12 years old. His life story began one night in June, on the eastern coast of Florida. First, Loggerhead's mother swam from the ocean and crawled up a sandy beach. Her flippers were not built for crawling, and she could not raise her big shell from the ground. But she struggled until she came to a place where waves could not splash and wet the sand. There she bent her hind paddles into scoops and dug a hole 10 inches deep. She laid 80 round white eggs in the hole and covered them with sand. Then she crawled back to the ocean and swam away.

The eggs took six weeks to hatch. The baby loggerheads scrambled out of the sand soon after midnight. They did not know about the ocean or how to get there, but instinct made them walk downhill and away from the dark trees near the beach. Soon a pair of raccoons saw the young turtles and caught a dozen of them just as they reached the water. Many more were eaten by hungry fish that were hunting near shore. Still, a few baby turtles escaped these mishaps and began to grow.

No one knows just where young loggerheads spend the first years of their lives. Do they stay in shallow water near the beaches where they hatched from eggs? Do they swim far out to sea, where no one can see them? Do they hide among water weeds in bays where rivers flow into the ocean? We only know that loggerheads that are 20 inches long and three to four years old are found in all these places. They also swim into swampy creeks, and sometimes they are found in harbors among fishing boats and ships.

As Loggerhead grew older and larger, he began to travel. Sometimes he swam out into the ocean until he was many miles from shore. At other times he wandered northward to the coasts of Georgia and South Carolina. Now and then he chased fish into bays and rivers, for fish were his favorite food. Soon he came back to the ocean, where he dived for the big snails known as whelks. Loggerhead crushed their shells with his beak and then swallowed their flesh.

One spring day when the turtle was 12 years old, he swam eastward across the Atlantic Ocean. For many miles the water was cool, and it looked greenish. Then the ocean began to feel warm, and soon it became so clear that it seemed blue, like the sky. The water also was flowing northward. When Loggerhead stopped swimming and went to sleep, the water carried him along at a speed of two miles per hour.

Although Loggerhead did not know what had happened, he had come into the Gulf Stream. This is a broad current that flows like a river through the Atlantic Ocean. The current is made of water that comes around the tip of Florida. It goes northward for many miles, swings eastward, and then flows across the ocean. Some of its warm water reaches the coast of England, Norway, and other parts of Europe.

Day after day the Gulf Stream carried Loggerhead northward. Sometimes he swam along with the current. At other times he floated or wandered about hunting fish. For a long time, he stayed far out in the ocean. When he did leave the Gulf Stream and travel toward shore, he came into Long Island Sound. Without counting his side trips after fish, he had traveled about 1,400 miles.

Long Island Sound was very different from the clear, quiet Gulf Stream. Near shore there were yachts with white sails, and other boats with noisy motors. Excursion vessels were crowded with people on vacations. Other boats carried fishermen who also were out for fun.

A man on one of the fishing boats first spied Loggerhead. "Look at the big turtle!" he shouted. "Captain, can't we go closer and get some pictures of him?"

Loggerhead noticed the boat and watched it turn toward him. At first he was not alarmed. But when the boat came closer, he dived and swam toward the open ocean. He kept on swimming until he reached the waters east of Florida.

The hawksbill turtle can be recognized by its overlapping scutes.

Several kinds of turtles live in warm oceans around the world. Atlantic loggerheads are most common near Florida and the West Indies, but they range as far southward as Brazil and eastward to the Mediterranean Sea. Pacific loggerheads, which are slightly different, are commonest near the western coast of Mexico. Both kinds sometimes crawl onto beaches to sun themselves, as well as to lay their eggs.

Green turtles may grow larger than loggerheads, but their heads are small. Their front flippers are long and oarlike, and usually have only one claw. The name of these turtles comes from the color of their fat. Thousands are caught and sold in markets, for their flesh makes a very popular soup. Most of the green turtles sold in markets are young, for they weigh less than 70 pounds.

Green turtle

Leatherback

Two ocean-dwelling turtles
The leatherback is the largest of all turtles. The green
turtle is smaller but better known, for it is used to make
soup.

Hawksbills are small sea turtles, for their shells are about two feet long. Hawksbills can be recognized by their scutes, which overlap like shingles.

Leatherback turtles are bigger than any other species. Their tough shells become six to eight feet long, and the whole reptile may weigh 700 to 900 pounds. The shell is marked by lengthwise ridges and is dark brown or brown spotted with yellow. The front flippers are so large that they look like wings.

These turtles wander southward as far as the coasts of Argentina and southern Africa. They also travel northward to Canada, the British Isles, and Japan. The females go ashore to lay eggs, but at other times these big reptiles swim far out in the ocean. They also seem to be rare, though no one really knows how many leatherbacks there are.

·   ·   ·

Garter snakes often swim in lakes or in bays along the sea coast. But real sea-dwelling snakes are poisonous reptiles that live in shallow offshore waters of the Indian and Pacific Oceans. The tails of sea snakes are flattened like oars. Nostrils are on the top of the snout; they close tightly and shut out water when the serpents dive. Like all reptiles, sea snakes breathe with lungs. This means that they must come to the surface to get air. They also like to bask in the sun by floating at the surface of the sea.

The yellow-bellied sea snake swims farther out to sea than its relatives do. It is also the only species that comes near North America, for it may be seen off the western coast of Mexico. This snake sometimes grows to be three feet long. It is black on top and yellow below, with a black-and-yellow spotted tail.

The yellow-bellied sea snake sometimes comes to the Pacific coast of Mexico.

Some young sea snakes are born in the water, but others hatch from eggs. Their mothers wriggle ashore and bury their eggs, as turtles do. All sea snakes feed on fish, which they kill with their venom. The reptiles almost never bite people.

There are no truly sea-dwelling lizards. Big black iguanas of the Galapagos Islands do dive and swim to get their food, which is seaweed. But these lizards never go far from shore, and they come back to land as soon as they finish their meals. Like sea snakes, they swim with their flattened tails. These iguanas can go more than an hour without breathing. This means that they do not have to come up for air while they are eating their meals.

Several kinds of crocodiles live in salt-water bays or at the mouths of swampy rivers. These reptiles often swim out to sea. Most of them soon go back to their rivers or bays, but the big

The Galapagos sea lizard is a black iguana that feeds on seaweed.

salt-water crocodiles of southeastern Asia are more daring. They often swim from island to island, and they sometimes take long trips. One of these reptiles swam more than 600 miles to an island in the Indian Ocean. Others travel almost 1,200 miles to the Fiji Islands, in the South Pacific.

Useful Reptiles

PITU, a bull snake, crawled over the ground in a cornfield. His body made a rustling sound as it rubbed against cornstalks and dry weeds. His tongue flicked out and then in to catch odors. They came from the ground, from plants, and from insects. But not one odor came from a creature that a bull snake would want to eat!

Pitu left the cornfield and began to cross a pasture. There he moved his head from side to side, so he could look as well as smell. When he spied a mound of fresh dirt, he crawled toward it. As he came near, his tongue caught the odor of a pocket gopher.

Pocket gophers are burrowing animals related to ground squirrels. When a gopher digs his underground tunnels, he pushes loose dirt to the surface. There the dirt piles up in mounds often called "gopher hills." The gopher fills the opening, or door, of his tunnel with still more dirt. Then he goes back and digs another load.

The bull snake had hunted gophers so often that he knew just how to do it. First he pushed his head into the hill and through the dirt that filled the door. Then he curved his neck sidewise and pulled some of the dirt to the surface. Pitu did this

Pitu, a bull snake, in a cornfield.

again and again, till the door was open. Then the snake crawled through it and glided into the tunnel.

Underground burrows protect pocket gophers from hawks, owls, weasels, and even human beings. But the bull snake slipped easily through one long tunnel and then another. At last he found the gopher. She sat where the second tunnel divided, nibbling a piece of potato.

The gopher had brought her food from a field just beyond the pasture. She had dug a long tunnel into the field, and had pulled several potatoes out of the ground. She ate a small one at once, but the others were much too big for one meal. The gopher bit them into small pieces, which she tucked into pockets in her cheeks. Then she stored the pieces in the tunnel where Pitu found her. She could eat the potatoes when she felt hungry but did not want to dig for food.

As Pitu came near, the gopher stopped eating and tried to run away. The bull snake caught her easily, wrapped himself around her, and squeezed until she was dead. Then he took hold of her head and began to swallow. The gopher's body was bigger than Pitu's, but his jaws spread so wide that he swallowed her without any trouble.

When the gopher had slid through Pitu's throat, he crawled to one door of the burrow. He pushed his nose out through the dirt, but he did not leave the tunnel. It was a cool, safe place in which to hide while he digested his meal.

Pocket gophers eat corn, wheat, potatoes, and other useful crops. The animals also spoil hayfields, eat bulbs of flowers, and kill fruit trees by gnawing their bark. Some scientists think the gophers do fifty million dollars' worth of damage every year.

Farmers kill pocket gophers with traps and poisons. But these methods take time and are expensive. It is much easier to let bull snakes and king snakes eat the gophers. The snakes also catch mice, rats, and ground squirrels. Ranchmen and farmers who know this protect the reptiles. Some people even gather bull snakes and turn them loose in their farms.

Bull snakes and their relatives have small heads and stout bodies as much as nine feet long. Common bull snakes are orange or reddish yellow with dark spots, but the pine snake is white and black. Pacific bull snakes are yellowish brown with square reddish-brown or black spots. Snake charmers often keep large bull snakes in side shows. Most of these reptiles come from Texas.

Bull snakes are not venomous, for they have no poison glands or fangs. Still, some people are afraid of them and even call them rattlesnakes. One reason for this is the bull snake's courage. Instead of gliding away when it is attacked, it may coil up and strike or bite. It may also shake its tail rapidly, which makes a rustling sound in dead leaves. Bull snakes are often killed because people think this rustling sound must be made by rattlesnakes.

• • •

Bull snakes are useful because they kill pocket gophers, rats, mice, and rabbits. But many other snakes also feed on destructive animals. These reptiles are worth more to farmers than poison or steel traps.

All rat snakes catch rats and mice, though they also eat eggs and small birds. Some species hunt in barns, sheds and corn cribs, but others remain outdoors. Corn snakes are the most brightly colored members of the group. Their sides are pale red or reddish brown, with crimson spots that have dark borders. Gray rat snakes are gray and white with black blotches, but fox

Pitu found the pocket gopher in its burrow.

snakes are yellowish and dark brown. The yellow rat snake is either yellow or brown, with four dark stripes from its neck to its tail. This serpent is often called the chicken snake, for it sometimes crawls into hen houses and eats eggs.

King snakes kill ground squirrels, mice, and other small animals. King snakes also swallow rattlesnakes and other poisonous species. The king snakes are able to do this because they are not harmed by venom. This is very strange, for rattlesnakes can kill each other. They also die if they bite themselves, as they sometimes do in fights.

Large king snakes sometimes swallow hens' eggs, just as chicken snakes do. But the milk snake does not drink milk or suck it from cows. This idea grew up long ago, probably because milk snakes hunted rats and mice in barns where cattle were fed and milked.

Racers eat mice and young rats, though they also like lizards, frogs, small snakes, and young birds. But no racer will attack large rattlesnakes, and racers never "charm" rabbits or birds. Although these snakes do little harm, they are not very useful to farmers.

• • •

Have you ever seen canned rattlesnake meat? It is safe to eat and it tastes good, though it is not a popular food. But lizards, tortoises, turtles, and turtle eggs are eaten in many parts of the world. Some have become such popular foods that they cost almost as much as snake meat.

Chuckawallas are large lizards that live in deserts of the Southwest. Indians once ate many chuckawallas after roasting

The corn snake kills many rats and mice.

or boiling the meat. Iguanas, which also are lizards, are eaten in southern Mexico, Central America, and some parts of South America. The reptiles are sold in village markets, along with chickens and pigs.

Green turtles, snapping turtles, and diamond-back terrapins are eaten in the United States. During the 1920's, diamond-back terrapins became so popular that they sold for $90 a dozen. Most terrapins are eaten in the South, but snapping turtle soup is popular in Philadelphia. Soup made with fat of the green turtle is eaten in many parts of the world.

Turtle eggs were once sold in the South, where they often were used in cakes. Both turtle meat and turtle eggs are common foods on many tropical islands. Unless fewer eggs are eaten and fewer turtles are killed, these reptiles will soon die out.

Countless thousands of giant tortoises once lived on the Galapagos Islands. Then, in the early 1800's, whaling ships became common in the Pacific Ocean. Whalers used the tortoises for food, since they were easy to catch and would live for months. The reptiles provided fresh meat and stew during long voyages for whales.

When whaling fell off, people began to kill the tortoises and make oil from their fat. Dogs and cats also were brought to the islands and were allowed to run wild. They soon learned to eat tortoise eggs and newly hatched babies, which have soft shells. All this made the reptiles scarce — so scarce that some varieties died out. Today, no one is allowed to kill the tortoises or use their flesh. Now and then, however, a few are taken to zoos.

Lizard skins and snakeskins are tanned for leather for belts, handbags, and women's shoes. Alligator skin is used, too, and is specially popular in handbags. The reptiles once were plentiful, but skin hunters killed so many that alligators became

The diamond-back terrapin is often used to make soup, especially in the South.

Baby alligators, such as this one, were once sold as pets.

scarce in many places. During one period of 15 years, skin hunters killed 2,500,000 alligators, just in Florida. No one knows how many alligators were shot in the rest of their range.

Tortoise shell does not come from tortoises. It is peeled from the shells of hawksbill turtles, which live in the sea. The peeled shell becomes soft when it is heated, and can be molded into various shapes. It once was made into combs and other ornaments. The ancient Romans even used it to veneer furniture.

Plastics have now taken the place of real "tortoise" shell. Plastic combs and frames for eyeglasses are often given tortoise-shell colors. Some people think the plastic products are not so beautiful as the actual shell, but they are much cheaper. They also keep turtles from being killed so their shells can be turned into ornaments.

Since reptiles are cold-blooded, they are not popular pets. Still, anole lizards are often sold at carnivals and fairs as "American chameleons." Few people know how to care for these little lizards, and most of them soon die. Baby alligators met the same fate in the days when they too were caught and sold as curios. Fortunately, when skin hunters killed too many grown alligators, laws were passed that stopped the sale of young ones.

It is not wrong to kill reptiles and use their skins or flesh, providing enough are left to keep the species from dying out. It also is not wrong to keep reptiles as pets if one takes good care of them. This means that they should have the right kinds of pens or cages, and just the right amount of heat to keep them happy and healthy.

Several books tell how to take care of pet reptiles. Some can be kept indoors for years, but others may be kept for a while and then turned loose. One of the best ways to know and enjoy reptiles is to keep kinds that live naturally near your home. After you have watched your pets for several weeks, turn them loose in places where they can live. In this way you can know and enjoy your reptile neighbors without doing them harm.

Index

Ages of reptiles, 79-80
Alligator, 15, 23, 45, 57-59, 122, 123
  in winter, 85
  nesting, 68
  range, 95
Alligator lizard, 47-49, 93
Amphibians, 11-13
Anole lizard, 15, 44, 51, 62-63

Ball python, 34, 54
Basilisk, 43, 44
Black racer, 20, 37, 81-85, 95
Blacksnake, common, *see* black racer
  pilot, 37-40, 67, 68, 69
Boa constrictor, 6, 41
Box turtle, 19, 64-66, 80
Brooding, 67-68

Camouflage, 49-51
Chameleons, American, 15, 44, 51, 52,
  62-63
  true, 24, 31, 32, 44, 52
Chuckawalla, 24, 26, 54, 120
Cobra, king, 21, 61
  spectacled, 55
  spitting, 56
Collared lizard, 42, 43
Color changes, 51-53
Constrictors, 6, 20, 21, 23, 41
Copperhead, 49, 51
Corn snake, 119, 121
Courtship, 59-63
Crocodiles, 23, 45, 57, 88, 95, 114
Crocodilians, defined, 15

Dermis, 7

Desert night lizard, 96
Desert tortoise, 19, 26, 86-88, 104
Diamond-backed rattlesnake, desert,
  104
  eastern, 35, 52, 53
Diamond-back terrapin, 121, 122

Ears, 33
Egg-eating snakes, 22, 23
Eggs and nests, 64-71
Embryo, 70, 71
Epidermis, 7, 9, 12, 15
Estivation, 87-88
Eyes, 29-32

Fangs, 75, 76
Feeling, 32-33, 36
Fence lizards, 89-92, 93
Flying dragon, 45

Galapagos tortoises, 60, 97-98, 121-122
Garter snakes, 7-11, 20, 60
Gecko, 43, 67
  ground, 30-31
  tokay, 44
Gila monster, 25, 26
Glass "snake," 43
Granite night lizard, 96
Green turtle, 19, 111, 112

Habitats, 95, 97
Hawksbill turtle, 111, 113, 123
Hearing, 33
Heat, shelter from, 86-88
Hibernation, 83-84, 86
Hog-nosed snake, 50, 52

Horned lizards, 53, 106
  regal, 102
  Texas, 99-101

Iguana, common, 6, 121
  Galapagos, 24, 114, 115
Indian python, 21

Jacobson's organs, 35
Jaws of snakes, 22-23
King snakes, 20, 49, 120
Komodo dragon, 34, 35

Lacerta, 32
Larvae, 11, 13
Leatherback turtle, 112, 113
Leopard lizard, 27-29, 31
Lizards, defined, 14
Loggerhead turtle, 107-111

Mastigure, spiny, 105
Monitors, 34-36
Mud puppy, 13, 15
Mud turtle, 14, 16
Musk turtle, 18

Odor trails, 59-60

Pacific turtle, 95
Painted turtle, 14, 16
Pilot blacksnake, 37-40, 67, 68, 69
Pit vipers, 36
Prairie rattlesnake, 73-78
Pythons, 20, 21, 34, 54, 67

Ranges, 19, 93-98
Rat snakes, 20, 119-120
Rattlesnakes, 21, 35, 36, 40
  defense, 52-55
  rattle, 77
  venom, 21, 75-76
Reptiles, defined, 12
Rubber boa, 54, 55

Salamanders, 11-12
Sand lizard, 103
Scales, 8, 12, 14, 39
Scutes, 13, 14, 15
Sea lizard, 114, 115
Sea snakes, 113, 114
Senses, 29-36
Shovel-nosed snake, 42, 84
Sidewinder, 40, 41, 95, 104
Sight, 29-32
Skink, western, 43
Smell, 34-35
Snakes, defined, 14
  feeding, 25
  sizes, 78
  swimming, 42, 113-114
  trails, 39, 41, 84
  young, 69, 72
Snapping turtle, alligator, 18
  common, 16-19, 50, 69, 93
Soft-shelled turtles, 18, 19
Speeds of reptiles, 46

Tadpoles, 11, 13
Tails, loss of, 48-49
Taste, 29, 34
Territory, 90, 92
Tortoises, 13, 45, 54, 60, 79, 121-122
Tuatara, 79, 97, 98
Turtles, 13, 14, 19, 45, 107-113,
  121-122

Undulatory motion, 38, 42
Uta, Colorado, 103

Venom, 21, 75-76
Vine snake, 31, 50
Vipers, 40, 84
Vision, types of, 31-32

Zebra-tailed lizard, 63, 103, 105, 106